NEW ENGLAND'S ROADSIDE ECOLOGY

NEW ENGLAND'S ROADSIDE ECOLOGY

EXPLORE 30 OF THE REGION'S UNIQUE NATURAL AREAS

THOMAS WESSELS

TIMBER PRESS + PORTLAND, OREGON

To Marcia, my constant companion for so many explorations over the past 53 years.

Frontispiece: Paper birch growing on the fringe of the Great Meadow, Acadia National Park, Maine.

Published in 2021 by Timber Press, Inc.

The Haseltine Building
133 S.W. Second Avenue, Suite 450
Portland, Oregon 97204-3527
timberpress.com

Printed in Thailand

MIX
Paper from responsible sources
FSC
www.fsc.org   FSC™ C136333

Text design by Hillary Caudle
Cover design by Amanda Weiss

ISBN 978-1-64326-009-9

A catalog record for this book is available from the Library of Congress.

CONTENTS

INTRODUCTION

This is a book of trail explorations that begin at a roadside stop, then take you into extraordinary natural places. My focus is on unique, interesting, beautiful ecological communities that most people might miss just walking along a trail.

There are so many fascinating and accessible ecosystems in New England! This book will lead you to and through unusual forests—such as old-growth stands and one thicket containing the tallest trees in the Northeast—as well as exquisite bogs, swamps, alpine tundra, and dunes. Each community is interpreted and its unique features along the trail are called to your attention. Photographs are incorporated to help people find noteworthy features.

All sites chosen for this book have well-developed trails or boardwalks that are open to the public. Trail lengths for the 30 sites vary from .5 to 4 miles, although most are between 1 and 2 miles. The majority of routes are of gentle to moderate difficulty, to accommodate a wide range of visitors. At the beginning of each chapter, you will find a short headnote about the site, its general location, and the difficulty and length of the hike. Specific locations, maps, directions, and additional information about the sites are easily found in a simple online search.

To help you learn the stories behind what you see on these hikes, there is a chapter following this introduction called "Features Focus: Explanations of Common Natural Characteristics." The entries in that chapter explain interesting features and conditions that occur frequently in our region and how to interpret them. I refer to this as reading the landscape. It's what I taught to graduate students, and I've been interpreting our northeastern landscapes for many years. I encourage you to read these explanations before you visit any area, because they contain significant facts about the organisms in our natural places—evidence to interpret the natural history of our region—and also because the features they describe are found in many of the explorations included here. At the beginning of each chapter thereafter, look for "Features Focus" in the heading, which will list the noteworthy aspects of the site that are covered in more detail in this special chapter, as well as corresponding page numbers.

In writing this book, I had to grapple with the reality that it could boost visitation rates to these areas, possibly increasing the adverse impacts of foot traffic. It is a risk. But I decided that helping people explore these extraordinary spots might help them forge stronger bonds with the natural world, and develop a greater level of respect and stewardship—and those potential benefits outweighed the risks. But I pledged to help mitigate any impacts by stressing good hiker etiquette. So I implore you to help protect these special places by staying on designated trails. Many of the areas are quite fragile and off-trail traipsing will quickly degrade them. Recently I did a site visit at Orono Bog—one of the sites shared in this book. It has a terrific boardwalk and yet I was disheartened to see that visitors had trampled the vegetation within 2 feet of the walkway. My guess is that they wanted to get closer to flowering plants to take photographs. Sadly (and ironically), if the visitors had just walked a bit farther down the boardwalk, the flowers they were seeking were growing right next to it.

I find that children develop hiker etiquette far quicker than adults. Granite outcrops are ecosystems to which I am very drawn, but they have fragile crevice and depression communities. When I tell children to only step on the granite and nowhere else, they instantly get it. Their parents, however, often have to be reminded. Most people have become so used to hiking on trails that they don't think about where they should place their feet, even when this awareness could protect fragile plants along a trail. So: if you have trouble remembering to stay on a trail and off its bordering vegetation, consider taking a child with you. Teach them good trail etiquette, and they will not let you forget it.

FEATURES FOCUS

This chapter offers deeper explanations and additional information on common aspects of the natural areas you will find in this book and throughout New England. The features here include the good, the bad, and the ugly: the amazing systems and interrelationships that organisms form to survive; explanations of how some life forms can have detrimental effects on other life forms in the quest to survive; and details of how even when life forms don't survive, life emerges from death in new and interesting ways. These are the clues to what has happened and continues to happen in our regional ecosystems.

As you browse the hikes and explorations in this book, look for "Features Focus" in the chapter heading, which will list the noteworthy aspects of the site that are covered in more detail here.

Basal Fire Scars

Tree wounds known as basal fire scars can be seen on many trees in natural areas of our region. Such a scar occurs at the base of a large trunk and is evidence that the tree survived a burn. These were spots where piles of leaves, sticks, branches, and other material had accumulated, providing fuel that burned long enough to kill the cambial tissue under the bark of the tree. The fire didn't burn through the bark, but a few years after the cambial tissue died, the bark fell away from the trunk and created the scar.

An uphill basal scar occurs when trees are growing on a slope. As forest debris moves downhill, tree trunks stand in the way of this flow. This material piles up on the uphill side of an obstructing trunk, while the tree's downhill side remains clear. If a fire is sparked and burns upslope, it runs right past the clear downhill side of a tree, but when it hits the combustible pocket on the uphill side, it burns there far longer. As with any basal scar, the heat then kills the cambial tissue beneath the bark and a scar eventually forms on the tree's uphill side. Any slope with a number of trees that have scars like this on their uphill side has likely been burned in the past.

An example of a basal scar on a northern white cedar tree. ▸

Beech Bark Scale

This disease is the result of an exotic scale insect that came to the New World on a load of European beech logs shipped to Nova Scotia in the late 1800s. The scale insect resides on the bark and feeds on the sap of beech trees, covering itself in a white, waxy coating to protect it from desiccation. It appears as a little white dot on the bark of beech trees. Eventually, as the number of scales on a tree increases, they compromise the tree's bark, allowing *Neonectria* fungi to invade. These fungi eventually weaken the trunk of a beech to the point where it will just break off, in what is called beech snap, killing the aboveground portion of the tree, but not its root system. Because beech is our only native interior forest tree that root-sprouts, as the trunk of the tree dies, it is replaced by root sprouts that also will eventually succumb to the disease. After a number of outbreaks, the beech trees in a stand become replaced by a dense understory of root sprouts. These form what is known as a "beech hell." Historically, beech trees were the most common representatives of northern hardwood old-growth stands, but this disease has dramatically changed the composition of this type of old growth.

Unfortunately, we have a number of introduced, exotic pathogens impacting our native trees. I am hopeful that, due to the workings of coevolution, the vast majority of our native trees will be okay, given time. The only exception is the beech. Studies show that somewhere in the range of 2 to 5 percent of beech trees are resistant to the impact of this disease. However, as beech hells develop, they expand outward, increasing the area of a forest understory that they dominate. Due to the dense network of roots and deep shade that develop in a beech hell, nothing else can establish within them. This means that through time, the number of seedlings from resistant trees will likely decrease as beech hells increase their dominance of the understory. Without intensive management, not only will

▲ Beech tree scale insects can be seen here as small white dots and marks on the bark. This tree is in the Dry River Old Growth ecosystem of New Hampshire.

resistant beech decline, but the total plant diversity in these stands will wither, making this a serious situation for our regional northern hardwood forests. Yet there is one hope. If one of our native species adapts to prey upon the scale insect—a potentially easy target since it is sedentary—the impact of this disease could decline and the beech would be given a fighting chance.

Chestnut Blight

Chestnut blight may have had the greatest single impact on the ecology of North America's eastern temperate deciduous forest in thousands of years. Around 1900, the chestnut blight fungus was accidentally introduced to North America with the importing of Asian chestnuts. These trees from Asia had coevolved with the fungus to the point that it was a mild parasite in its land of origin, but to the American chestnut, the new arrival was lethal. It is estimated that at the time of the introduction, American chestnut was one of the most common forest trees east of the Mississippi River. One out of every four trees was a chestnut in some Appalachian stands. These trees were also massive, with trunks up to 14 feet in diameter. They produced the most consumed nut in North America. American chestnut was truly the signature tree of the temperate deciduous forest, but in only 30 years, it was almost completely eradicated by the blight. Trees less than 10 inches in diameter had the ability to stump sprout after their trunks were girdled (when cambial tissue beneath bark is destroyed in a ring around the trunk) by the blight, but larger trees died outright, prompting massive salvage efforts for the highly sought-after wood.

Although the chestnut blight was a devastating blow, I am confident that in time—possibly hundreds or thousands of years— the American chestnut will come back. Whenever there is a strong selection pressure such as the chestnut blight—something that kills off a large percentage of a population—the surviving individuals are the ones that have some level of resistance. That doesn't mean they are not impacted, but they can reach reproductive age. Since 2012, I have encountered five stands of American chestnuts that display resistance and are reproducing with seedlings and saplings in the understory. These resistant trees will eventually succumb to the blight, but will also have decades of reproductive time before they do. Since the only trees reproducing have some degree of resistance and have to cross-pollinate to make viable nuts, each succeeding generation should have greater resistance than its predecessor. In time, we can hope they will coevolve with the fungus as they did in Asia.

Glacial Impact

Between around 90,000 and 20,000 years ago, a massive glacier called the Laurentide Ice Sheet covered most of northern North America, including all of New England. The ice was more than a mile deep in many places, and as the ice sheet advanced for tens of thousands of years, it scraped, gouged, eroded, and shaped many of the landscapes of our region. Exposed ridgelines, U-shaped valleys and cirques, and polished granite are just a few of the New England features that were created by the glacier. In fact, the massive weight of the ice even pushed the continental crust of our region hundreds of feet down, into the planet's mantle.

Then, 24,000 years ago, the Laurentide Ice Sheet began to melt and recede northward as the global climate warmed. The glacial ice sheet had collected all sorts of materials while it was advancing, from clay and sand to boulders and pebbles. As the glacier melted, these sediments and debris—called glacial till—were widely deposited across the landscape.

Evidence of the Laurentide Ice Sheet's advance and recession are visible on explorations throughout this book.

◄ Glacially polished granite shows striations: straight, parallel gouges that were etched as small rocks embedded in glacial ice scraped over bedrock.

Grafting

Many of our New England trees growing within 10 to 15 feet of each other become root grafted. This can happen within species, between species, and more strikingly, even between broad-leaved trees and conifers. If two trees have been root grafted and one is cut down, its stump can sometimes manage to survive from the energy of the other

▲ Two northern white cedars that grafted at their trunks' bases.

tree through the graft connection. Less often, trees can also graft trunk to trunk instead of through their roots. This occurs when the trees are growing very close to each other and repeatedly rub together and through their bark, allowing their cambial tissues to graft.

Great New England Hurricane of 1938

While it is not really a feature, but rather a natural event, the Great New England Hurricane of 1938 had a huge impact on the ecosystems of New England, and visibly affected five of the sites covered in this book. It was a very powerful—possibly category 4—storm that was unusual because of the high speed with which it traversed New England. It made landfall near New Haven, Connecticut, around 3 p.m. Traveling at over 40 miles an hour, the hurricane was moving into Canada to the west of Lake Champlain a bit after 9 p.m. Because of its fast advance, it was also called the Long Island Express Hurricane. Its traveling velocity enabled the storm to maintain itself as a hurricane well into central Vermont, 200 miles from where it made landfall, causing a long path of forest blowdowns and widespread infrastructure damage. When the storm was in western Massachusetts, the Blue Hill Observatory just south of Boston—roughly 100 miles away—clocked 121-mile-an-hour sustained winds and one gust at 186 miles per hour.

Tragically, the storm was not predicted to make landfall in New England, so people flocked to the shore in places like Rhode Island to see the impressive surf. A storm surge of over 20 feet in many places rose within minutes of landfall. Close to 700 people died in the storm, the majority washed out to sea by the surge.

The sites covered in this book that were impacted by the hurricane were on the eastern side of the storm's path. They all received stand-leveling (the ability to level a stand of trees) winds from the southeast. Sites not covered in this book in adjacent New York State that were on the western side of the storm's path took damaging winds from the northeast.

Math in Nature

The Fibonacci sequence is one of the most well-known patterns in mathematics. It is a series of numbers in which each number is the sum of the two numbers that precede it—for example, 0, 1, 1, 2, 3, 5, 8, and 13 are part of the sequence. Once the number 5 is reached in the series, each succeeding pair of numbers will create a ratio that slightly fluctuates around .617. This is known as the golden mean. For example, the ratio of 5 to 8 is .625, and 8 to 13 is .615. These concepts go beyond math, however. They are common patterns in nature, and can be detected in all the natural areas covered in this book.

For example, lenticels are portals for trees to absorb carbon dioxide into their bark to conduct bark photosynthesis. Visible on younger balsam fir trees in the Philbrick-Cricenti Bog exploration in New Hampshire, the lenticels are horizontal lines that appear on the bark. Looking closely at these lenticels, you will see that each one is the juncture of a clockwise and counterclockwise spiral. If you count the number of clockwise spirals of lenticels going around a tree and then count the number of counterclockwise spirals, you will always get two consecutive numbers in the Fibonacci sequence.

In fact, all interlocking right-hand and left-hand spirals found in nature are based on two consecutive numbers in the Fibonacci series. This is not just true

▲ These pitch pine cones show interlocking spirals of scales that are mathematically connected.

for balsam fir lenticels, but for scales in pitch pine cones, the seed pattern in the head of a sunflower, and an endless number of natural examples. Single spirals in nature also are based on this series. Find a drawing of a nautilus shell, draw both a vertical and horizontal line through its center (dissecting the shell into 4 equal quarters), then measure the arch of the shell's spiral in each succeeding quarter. You will consistently get a ratio of .617 by dividing the length of the shorter arch by the longer one that follows it.

Even our bodies are structured on the Fibonacci sequence. Some time when you are with a group of a couple dozen people, measure the length from their elbows to their middle fingers. Average those measurements. Then do the same for the length from their shoulders to their middle fingers. The ratio of the first average number to the second average number will be .617. The Fibonacci series abounds in nature and there is an active debate about why this is so. My guess is that it just may be an easy developmental pathway to follow.

Old Growth

Old growth is generally defined as a stand of trees that has reached maximal age without experiencing any form of disturbance during its tenure. Depending on species, in New England this means trees that are between 250 and 700 years old. Stands of old-growth trees are increasingly rare in our region, but efforts to preserve such important links to nature's past are growing.

Pillows and Cradles

Observing the surficial ground topography of our forests, there are often visible differences—sometimes in areas adjacent to each other. The ground on one side of an old stone wall is smooth on its surface, while the ground the other side looks lumpy. The lumpy ground is the result of live trees being uprooted. The crater left by a downed tree's extensive root system and any attached soil and rocks is known as a cradle or pit. As the roots and trunk decay over time, the soil and stones that were clinging to the root mass form a pile on the ground, known as a pillow or mound. Areas like this found years later suggest that the site has either always been forested or is an abandoned pasture. When pillows and cradles are *not* present, the ground is visibly even, and a stone wall is nearby, it is usually proof that at some point, the area was plowed, removing the pillows and cradles to create a hayfield or crop field.

Stone Walls and Early Agriculture

When the British first colonized New England, one of the things that amazed them was the soil. For thousands of years, soil organisms excavating material to the surface had only brought up fine materials, eventually burying the rock of glacial till under a good foot of stone-free soil.

The colonist farmers who created hayfields here needed to plow just a few times, to remove the pillows and cradles and make the ground level for harvesting with a scythe. The perennial roots of the hay then wove everything in the soil together, preventing rocks slowly moving to the surface during freeze-thaw cycles.

▲ Pillows and cradles are formed by trees that were downed and uprooted long ago.

▲ Among the large stones that anchor this rock wall are many smaller stones removed from the once-adjacent crop field.

However, in crop fields that had no perennial roots, buried rocks began moving vertically in the freezes and thaws of the seasons. After a decade or so, these fields started turning up rocks, including a lot of fist-sized stones that needed to be removed. These rocks were cleared and added to stone walls anchored by larger rocks, or simply gathered in piles.

In areas solely used as pasture for livestock, large stones and boulders that could be problematic were removed and used in stone walls, but lumpy ground with pillows and cradles was not a problem and was left as it was.

What is the lesson for interpreting natural lands that were once agricultural? A smooth-grounded area bordered by a stone fence with telltale mug-sized rocks suggests that crops were grown there. Stone fences that lack the fist-sized rocks and have adjacent smooth topography suggest that the fence was once adjacent to a hayfield. Lumpy terrain with pillows and cradles and an adjoining stone wall was an early livestock pasture.

Stump Sprouts

Hardwoods and our regional pitch pines have a special survival technique. If they are cut or burned, but retain a stump and root system (even if the trunk is killed), epicormic buds that lie dormant under the bark of the stump will sprout when the bark is exposed to additional light. These sprouts can then grow into new trunks, accounting for a tree with multiple trunks. The original stump then decays away and leaves only a multi-trunked tree.

This red maple's original trunk was burned in a 1947 fire, then sent up stump sprouts that became the multiple trunks seen here. ▸

Tipped Trees

A tipped tree is one that is still living but instead of growing straight up, the bottom of its trunk is at an angle. Usually, farther up the angled portion of the trunk, there is an elbow and the trunk turns and grows upward. These trees were tipped by strong winds when they were young. The vertical trunk after the elbow was the lowest living limb on the tree when it was tipped. This limb then became the new trunk. Generally, only small trees, with trunks less than 6 inches in diameter, are vulnerable to being tipped like this. Larger trees get tipped as well, but as they lean over, they often develop so much momentum that they crash to the ground, completely uprooted.

Trees can also be bent over by the weight of snow and ice loading, or a neighboring tree falling on them. Trees bent in this fashion have trunks that are shaped like a bow.

A somewhat related term is "tip-up," which refers to the often sizable base and root mass of a tree that has been completely toppled. This mass can often reach large dimensions and rise many feet into the air.

▲ This maple tree is a good example of what happens when a tree is tipped and the lowest limb takes over as the main trunk.

▲ A large, uprooted tree base and root mass is called a tip-up.

Tree Secrets

BLACK BIRCH

Black birch has bark that, as it ages, goes through distinct changes in texture. The first stage is smooth, black bark with many horizontal, white lenticels (portals for a tree to absorb carbon dioxide into its bark for photosynthesis). All trees with young bark have lenticels, though they are easier to spot on some species than others. If you find a black birch with live twigs, scrape a section of twig with your fingernail and you will see that just under the bark is a green layer of chlorophyll. If its roots are not ice bound, a tree with photosynthetic bark can do photosynthesis at temperatures below freezing, extending the tree's growing season.

At about 50 years old, the smooth bark of the black birch starts to develop vertical fissures. Around 80 years old, the bark starts curling away from these fissures to develop rectangular-shaped plates. At approximately 150 years of age, these rectangular plates are usually shed, allowing the birch to once again have smooth-looking bark, now without lenticels. As the birch approaches 200 years old, it starts developing vertical bark ridges and begins looking more like an older red oak.

When you scrape a black birch twig to see its chlorophyll layer, smell the exposed chlorophyll. You'll catch the fragrant scent of wintergreen, whose technical name is methyl salicylate. Large quantities of methyl salicylate can be a strong irritant, and in black birch, it wards off browsing by animals such as deer.

BLACK GUM

Black gum, also known as tupelo, is a southern swamp tree finding its northern range limits in southern Vermont and New Hampshire. The region's scattered black gum swamps are refugia (areas of unaltered climate and persistent organisms) from a time when they were more widely distributed, about 8000 years ago.

Black gum swamps typically develop on fens—wetlands that, like bogs, develop peat but are less acidic. Fens are dominated by species of sphagnum moss and sedges. In the northern states of

New England, black gum swamps are usually found on ridgetops—like the Vernon black gum swamp in Vermont—rather than the more commodious valley locations. The reason? Strong ridgetop winds are not as threatening to the black gum—even those perched on mucky peat—as wind is to other trees.

▴ A contorted black gum, in the Vernon Black Gum Swamp in Vermont, has been broken multiple times—as can be seen in the many elbows of its trunk—but has never been uprooted.

The black gum is a more highly evolved swamp tree than our other regional species, with adaptations that help it survive strong winds. Black gums have very brittle wood that also tends to develop heart rot, creating trees with hollow trunks. When exposed to strong winds, their tops snap off, allowing their trunks to remain standing. Luckily, the black gum has lots of epicormic buds. These buds lie dormant under the bark of the trunk and will sprout new branches when the bark is exposed to additional light. When strong winds hit a swamp, our other regional swamp trees—such as red maple, yellow birch, spruce, and eastern hemlock—completely topple, while the black gum trunks remain standing and then resprout new branches below their snap-off points.

NORTHERN WHITE CEDAR

Northern white cedars are interesting in a number of ways. They can grow in an array of diverse conditions, from saturated fens (wetlands that develop peat but are less acidic than bogs), to very dry and nutrient-deprived granite outcrops, to dry and enriched limestone environments. I know of no other tree species that can tolerate such extremes in moisture and pH. Northern white cedar is the oldest-growing tree species in the northeastern states, with individuals along the shore of Lake Superior dated at 1200 years. These cedars also vigorously root graft with their neighboring trees; often the aboveground grafted roots between two trees are visible. They are also hit by lightning strikes more frequently than any other species of our regional trees. If you see a spiraling scar on the trunk of a northern white cedar, it was produced by lightning. Finally, all other regional conifers have wood that rots from the outside in. That is not the case with northern white cedar, whose stumps and trunks hollow out. Since the outer wood of the cedar is highly rot resistant, hollow stumps of this species can persist for more than a century.

White Pine Weevil

White pines that are impacted by this weevil at some height—usually not more than 30 feet above ground—have their single trunk split into two or more trunks. This happens when the weevil lays its eggs on the uppermost terminal (end) shoot of a pine. The eggs hatch as larvae and drill into the terminal shoot, killing it. When this happens, limbs in the whorl (layer of branches) directly below the killed shoot take off and grow upward to replace the dead shoot. If a pine is growing by itself in full sunlight, all the limbs in the whorl below the top may grow up, giving that tree as many as five new trunks to replace the single one. If a dense stand of young white pines is being hit by the weevil, those trees only send up two of their limbs to become new trunks.

White pine weevils do not lay eggs on all white pine trees. They only choose young pines—generally less than 15 years of age—that are growing in full sunlight. These trees are targeted because the insects want a terminal shoot that is as thick as a finger, to serve as forage for their young. Older pines, or trees growing in shade, have terminal shoots that are usually only about .25 inches in diameter—too small to interest a weevil. This is a significant piece of evidence when interpreting landscape histories, because it reveals that a stand of weevil-impacted pines was the first cohort of trees to colonize a once-open site. If those trees are young enough, it becomes possible to date when they started growing by counting their limb whorls, because white pines produce only one whorl per year.

▲ Multiple trunks above the splits or forks in these white pines are clues that they were hit by weevils.

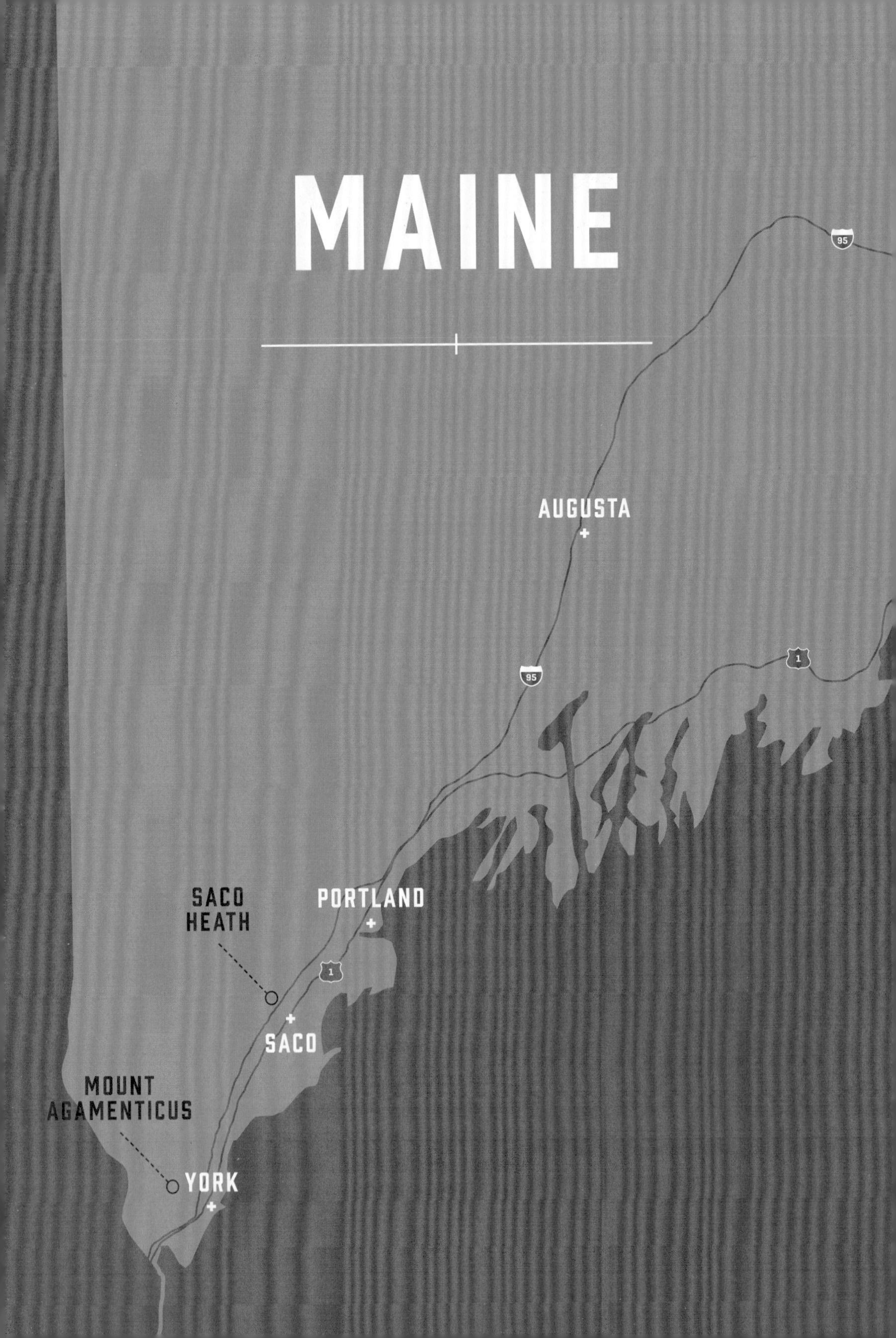

MAINE

95

AUGUSTA
+

95

1

SACO
HEATH

PORTLAND
+

1

+
SACO

MOUNT
AGAMENTICUS

YORK
+

ORONO
BOG

+ ORONO

BANGOR
+

GREAT WASS
ISLAND PRESERVE

BEALS
+
Great
Wass
Island

BAR HARBOR
+

Mt. Desert
Island

SIEUR DE
MONTS

GORHAM
MOUNTAIN

AREA OF DETAIL

1

SACO HEATH

A bog that has risen above the surrounding land

DIFFICULTY
Easy

LOCATION ▸ Saco, Maine
FEATURES FOCUS ▸ Glacial impact, old growth, stump sprouts

LENGTH
1.75 miles

The Saco Heath can be accessed via State Route 112, just a few miles northwest of Saco, Maine. During rainy periods, the beginning of the trail leading to the boardwalk may have some wet patches. A good time to visit the heath is from late May to early June, when the majority of its plants are in bloom.

Saco Heath is the most southerly raised bog found in eastern North America and, as such, is a very unusual ecosystem. All bogs create peat—partially decomposed plant material. A good amount of peat is derived from species of sphagnum moss. Peat can absorb large amounts of water and, as the water-dense peat builds up, it can raise the water table along with it. In a bog like Saco Heath, the center of the heath and its water table are actually higher in elevation than the surrounding woodlands, leading to the term "raised bog."

In 1986, the Joseph Deering family made a generous gift of the heath to The Nature Conservancy. The conservancy has done a great job of making this rare and fragile ecosystem open to the public, by building a half-mile-long boardwalk through it. Because of the boardwalk, large numbers of people can visit the heath each day and not impact the site; however, visitors need to stay on the designated trail from the parking lot to the boardwalk, which passes through a delicate swamp ecosystem.

Leaving the parking area, you'll enter a forest composed of white pine, hemlock, red oak, and red maple. Evidence of past logging in this forest can be seen in the many rounded, moss-covered mounds—the remnants of pine stumps—and frequent coppiced hardwood trees that have two or more trunks growing from one root system. Hardwoods like red maple and red oak will sprout new growth from dormant buds that become activated when the bark under which they reside receives increased sunlight. These are called epicormic buds, and when trees are cut and light is allowed in, these buds in the stump will sprout a number of new trunks.

As you continue down the trail, the environment will transition into a tree swamp—wetlands that are dominated by trees. In the understory you will find lots of royal and cinnamon ferns, the latter named for the color of the plant's central fertile frond. In time, the ground in the swamp will become too wet, and you will begin a wooded section of the boardwalk.

Just after the wooded section of the boardwalk ends and before you enter the open heath community, look to your right for a large, scarred hemlock. This tree was hit by a lightning strike prior to 1970. The timing of the strike can be ascertained by the mature bark that has grown on the callus wood attempting to grow over the scar. A close look at this wound will show that as you look up, it is spiraling to the left.

All trees are genetically determined to have their trunks grow in a spiral pattern. This is a part of their phyllotaxy (arrangement of leaves on a stem) that keeps limbs from growing directly above one

▲ Cinnamon fern is named for its central, light brown, fertile frond.

▲ A scar from an old lightning strike follows the leftward trunk spiral of this hemlock.

another. My observations suggest that most of our trees, regardless of species, spiral to the right as one looks up the trunk. This hemlock atypically spirals to the left. Although the direction of spiral is genetically programmed, the intensity of the spiral is determined by environment. If trees elongate their trunks quickly, it's like stretching a spring, and the intensity of the spiral is reduced. If the elongation is slower, the spiral is more intense—and the trunk is stronger. This is a particular advantage for wind-stunted trees, whose tight trunk spirals make breakage events unlikely. Others that have strong trunk spirals are open-grown trees that grow outward rather than upward, those that are canopy suppressed, and old-growth trees that have stopped increasing their height. Lightning strikes always follow the trunk spiral of trees, as happened with this hemlock. After passing the hemlock, you will quickly leave the forest canopy, step onto the boardwalk, and enter the Saco Heath—a bog community.

More than 15,000 years ago, after a continental glacier called the Laurentide Ice Sheet had retreated out of this part of Maine, the Saco Heath was a lake whose shoreline was kept free of marginal vegetation by wave action. Over many centuries, the lake filled with sediment and eventually became shallow enough that emergent aquatic plants—such as pond lilies, pondweeds, and rushes—started growing offshore. As the density of this vegetation increased, it dampened wave action to the point that the margin of the lake became vegetated as well, converting the lake to a pond. Based on qualities of the water in ponds, marginal vegetation can be one of three basic types: marsh, fen, or bog.

If the water is moderate in temperature, has ample nutrients, and is not acidic, marsh vegetation will develop, dominated by species such as cattails, sedges, and rushes. If the water in the pond is cold, acidic, and low in nutrients, bog vegetation will form, such as sphagnum moss and the heath-family shrub leatherleaf. If the pond water is somewhere in between these two extremes, fen vegetation will form—sphagnum moss and sedges such as cotton grass. Saco Heath's original pond was fed by cold spring water that was acidic and low in nutrients, supporting bog vegetation.

Bogs can form floating mats because of the buoyancy of the sphagnum that is stitched together by the roots of the leatherleaf. Floating mats like these are often called quaking bogs. The floating mat cuts off oxygen to the water underneath it and as vegetation dies and starts to decompose into peat, all the oxygen in the water under the mat can be consumed, creating an anaerobic environment. At this point the peat no longer decomposes and starts to build up under the mat.

Life can exist in the most extreme environments. Algae grow on the snowpack at the summit of Mount Everest. Whole ecosystems thrive under great pressure at 36,000 feet deep in the Pacific Ocean's Marianas Trench. Bacteria even grow in bedrock hundreds of feet below the surface. Yet in a bog, just a few feet under the mat, nothing lives. This is even more striking given that there is plenty of water, a huge energy resource in the peat, and it is a stable environment whose temperature fluctuates between 39 and 55 degrees F annually. Why can nothing live under a bog mat? With no oxygen and an acidic pH of 3.5, it is similar to conditions for pickling. This means that anything below the mat is preserved for millennia. In her book *Reading the Landscape of America*, May Watts has a chapter on bogs titled "History Book with Flexible Cover." It references the fact that pollen settling in bogs is preserved, allowing researchers to reconstruct changes in vegetation over thousands of years.

So—stepping onto the boardwalk, surrounded by a sea of leatherleaf, contemplate all the things that are perfectly preserved just a few feet down, including any animals that might have happened to fall through the bog mat. From stomach analyses of mammoths that drowned in bogs over 12,000 years ago, researchers can easily identify what the animal ate the day it perished.

▲ A boardwalk provides easy access to the Saco Heath bog.

Although leatherleaf is the prevailing shrub in the heath, there are a number of other shrubs that are also members of the heath family and grow a bit taller. These include rhodora, with its pink blossoms; sheep laurel, also with pink flowers; highbush blueberry, which has white bell-shaped blossoms; and Labrador tea, featuring white umbels and dense, brownish fuzz on the undersides of its leaves. Another member of the heath family you'll encounter is the small cranberry—vine-like with tiny leaves growing across the sphagnum mat. It is striking that such a small plant can produce such a large berry: sometimes almost an inch in diameter.

Many of these shrubs, such as leatherleaf, sheep laurel, small cranberry, and Labrador tea, have small, evergreen leaves to retain nutrients. If they shed their leaves in fall, like most of our broad-leaved woody plants do, the nutrients in those leaves would be leached out by the acidic bog environment and become unavailable for future uptake. Small leaf size helps reduce desiccation in winter, when the cold air has very low relative humidity levels.

As you move farther into the heath, you will encounter pitch pine as the dominant tree with lesser numbers of larch, white pine, gray birch, red maple, and black spruce. These trees are growing in areas where the peat is thick enough to keep the bog from quaking, giving them the support they need to remain standing. Bogs with pitch pine are quite rare in New England and the Saco Heath is one of the best examples of this ecological community.

▲ Highbush blueberry has white bell-shaped blossoms.

▲ Rhodora is known for pink blossoms.

▲ Labrador tea has white umbels.

All pine needles grow in clusters. White pine has five needles per cluster, the same number of letters in the word "white." Pitch pine has three needles per cluster, easily remembered by connecting "pitch" to baseball—3 strikes and you're out. It is believed that fire plays a role in bogs that support pitch pine because this species needs a good amount of light to establish; fires remove the shrub layer and create such light. With this in mind, The Nature Conservancy does controlled burns in the heath from time to time.

▲ Benches provide a spot to rest about half-way along Saco Heath's boardwalk.

▲ An old-growth pitch pine's large bark plates suggest the tree may have been there more than two centuries.

Pitch pine is undoubtedly the most fire-adapted tree in New England. Its rot-resistant needles build up a fuel source where the tree grows, encouraging hot fires that will remove faster-growing competitors. It also has especially thick bark, even when the tree is young, that protects it from the heat of fire. If the fire gets too hot for the bark to protect the tree, it can stump sprout below any areas damaged by heat—pitch pine is our only regional conifer that can do this. Farther south, such as in the Pine Barrens of New Jersey, pitch pines have developed serotinous cones—these are special cones that remain closed and only open when temperatures exceed 125 degrees F (during a fire), in order to time the tree's seed release with fires that will open germination sites. Serotinous cones hold viable seeds up to 25 years.

Pitch pines are commonly found in dry, acidic sites like the sandy substrates of Cape Cod or the granite domes of Acadia National Park. Why would they be growing in the Saco Heath, with its saturated substrates? Because the water of the heath is so acidic that the trees can't take up much of it. From the perspective of the tree, that makes this a xeric or dry site.

Halfway down the boardwalk, you will come to two benches that face each other. About 40 feet before the benches, on the right side of the boardwalk, is an ancient pitch pine that most likely exceeds 200 years of age. A look at this tree's bark plates will show that they are about 3 inches wide and 14 inches long. Bark plates of this size occur only on the oldest specimens of pitch pine. It is very likely that this tree started growing around 1800, or possibly even earlier, on a section of the heath that was stable enough to support it.

After the benches, the boardwalk continues on another quarter of a mile across the bog, ending at a small loop trail. The trail takes you through an island dominated by white pine and rises a few feet above the heath before reversing direction back to the parking area. Take your time on the return trip to fully enjoy this wetland.

SIEUR DE MONTS

Fire scars, a tree swamp, and peeling paper birch

DIFFICULTY

Easy

LOCATION ▸ Acadia National Park, Bar Harbor, Maine

FEATURES FOCUS ▸ Basal fire scars, old growth, stump sprouts

LENGTH

1.5 miles

The trail follows an old road and starts in Acadia National Park. It will take you through pockets of old-growth hemlock forest, younger hardwood forests generated by the Fire of 1947, and through the Great Meadows marsh. You'll return by boardwalk through a swamp where mostly red maple and birch trees grow. It is unusual to have such a mix of ecological communities in such close proximity.

Start at the Sieur de Monts spring, which was an inspiration to George Dorr, known as the "father of Acadia National Park." Dorr saw the spring as the heart of Acadia, which would become the first national park east of the Rocky Mountains. Radiating from the spring are a number of memorial paths built between 1913 and 1916 under the direction of Dorr. These paths boast some of the most impressive stonework among any hiking trails in the United States. For those who don't mind steep climbs, it is worthwhile to hike the nearby Beachcroft, Emery, or Homans Paths, which have wonderful stairways, terraces, and granite slab walkways.

From the spring, head north toward Jessup Path. Look to your left before you reach the path and you will see old sugar maples that were spared by the 1947 fire. The conflagration burned more than 17,000 acres on the east side of Mount Desert Island, including 10,000 acres of the park and many historic hotels and mansions. Immediately after the fire, people believed it would put an end to the growing tide of tourists that came each summer. In fact, just a few decades later, park visitation had increased as hikers were drawn to ridgeline trails with more open vistas. The fire also replaced a relatively homogeneous forest with one that is more diverse and quite striking during fall foliage season. It is no accident that more cruise ships come to Bar Harbor during October, when the foliage is at its best, than at any other time of year. Evidence of the fire can still easily be seen on this loop.

Once you reach Jessup Path, continue north a short distance until you join with Hemlock Road. At this point Jessup Path continues straight as a boardwalk, but you will turn slightly left and follow Hemlock Road. Before taking that left, look toward the boardwalk to see a fairly homogeneous stand of paper and gray birches. On the east side of Mount Desert Island, wherever stands of these birches or quaking and bigtooth aspens occur, conifer forests likely once grew, but were destroyed by the 1947 fire. In areas where hardwoods such as maple and oak burned, they returned as coppiced trees (from stump sprouts), while coniferous forests were killed outright. The exposed soil in these areas was a perfect germination site for the wind-dispersed, small seeds of birch and aspen.

Other signs of the fire along Hemlock Road are basal scars at the bases of large trees that survived the burn. These spots were piles of leaves, sticks, and branches that burned and killed the cambial tissue under the tree's bark. After the cambial tissue died, the bark fell from the trunk and the scar was left.

▴ This coppiced red oak stump sprouted following the Fire of 1947.

▴ A basal fire scar on a sugar maple. The bark didn't initially burn, but the cambium beneath was killed and the bark fell off later.

More remnants of the Fire of 1947 are stands of trees that show an age discontinuity. These are areas that have a lot of small trees and a few scattered large trees, but none of intermediate size. Fires create a forest structure like this, in which the only survivors are large trees with thick bark and a lot of thermal mass in their wood, or those that stump sprout later. Trees and shrubs of a smaller and intermediate stature were burned and killed.

▲ Age discontinuity, in which two older hemlocks are surrounded by younger trees.

As you continue down Hemlock Road, keep an eye out for large old hemlocks that survived the fire. These small pockets of old-growth trees can be seen where Hemlock Trail intersects Hemlock Road. After the trail intersection, Hemlock Road turns a bit to the right, and forest on both sides of the old road is replaced by swamp. Walking along this section, before you cross Jessup Path, compare the coppiced red maples on the left side of Hemlock Road with those on the right. You should notice that the ones on the right have much larger trunks. This is because the road acted as a firebreak. The trees on the left were consumed by the fire, which came racing in from the northwest, while those to the right were not impacted. The question then becomes why the larger red maples on the right are coppiced. The answer is that red maples growing in swamps *also* naturally stump sprout, even without the impetus of fire. They were stump sprouting before the fire, and therefore had a head start on the maples on the left, which were stump sprouted later by the fire.

After crossing Jessup Path, both sides of Hemlock Road become bordered by gray birches. I suspect they were intentionally planted and managed, because if they were simply an artifact of regeneration following the fire, there should be other tree species mixed in with the birch. These trees create an aesthetically pleasing walking path with framed views of the Great Meadow to the right.

The Great Meadow is a wet meadow—a marsh with a prevalence of sedge and grass species. For periods of the year, it has standing water. Long before the creation of Acadia National Park, the Great Meadow was likely a pond that, through time, slowly filled with

Gray birches border Hemlock Road as it passes through the Great Meadow. ▸

sediments and became a marsh. The same thing is happening today in the Tarn, also part of Acadia, which was a wet meadow prior to the establishment of the park. Dorr had the stream flowing out of the Tarn dammed to create a pond that is in the process of transitioning back to a marsh.

Hemlock Road intersects with Park Loop Road, which you will cross and then turn left on Great Meadow Loop Trail. In a short distance this will bring you to Jessup Path, where you will cross Park Loop Road heading back south. Just after you cross the road and start down Jessup Path, look up at the tops of the aspens. Can you see the bright orange maritime sunburst lichen? This lichen needs a good amount of calcium and can usually be found growing on the cement of stone walls or on seaside granite where gulls frequently perch and eliminate. Continuing down the trail, look to your right to see some old pitch pines, identified by their large bark plates, which survived the 1947 fire. Then the forest gives way to the Great Meadow again, with views to the right that look over the marsh toward the north ridgeline of Cadillac Mountain.

Down Jessup Path, the wet meadow will transition to a tree swamp composed of gray birch, red maple, and speckled alder. This occurs because the marsh here has filled with enough sediment and decomposed organic matter that the standing water has been

reduced and trees can invade. When you reach the boardwalk portion of Jessup Path, the swamp will have even less standing water. This in turn allows much larger red maples to predominate the swamp and cinnamon fern to grow in the understory. The wetland successional sequence you have walked through—from the open wet meadow adjacent to Hemlock Road to the start of the boardwalk on Jessup Path—has taken many centuries to develop, as sediment and organic matter gradually replaced water in the marsh.

On the Jessup Path boardwalk, look for more lichen growth on the trunks of trees. Lichens are formed by a mutualistic relationship between two species of fungus and a species of alga. This creates a single plantlike structure composed of up to three separate species. This is an obligatory relationship for the fungi that need their algal partner to survive. Although the algae can be free living, when they become lichenized, their populations expand by letting the algae colonize sites they couldn't without their fungal partners. Lichens that grow on trees form three basic groups based on morphology:

▲ This captivating scene looks over the Great Meadow to the north ridge-line of Cadillac Mountain.

▲ Jessup Path's boardwalk crosses the wetland.

▲ The red maple swamp lies at the north end of Jessup Path's boardwalk.

crustose lichens appear to be painted on surfaces, making a flat covering with no noticeable structures; foliose lichens look like leaves or lettuce; fruticose lichens have structures that grow up and away from the bark of trees.

For many years it was thought that lichens had what is known as a commensalistic relationship with the trees they grew upon. Commensalistic means one species obtains food or other benefits from another species without harming or benefitting the latter. In this case, it was thought lichens benefitted by growing on tree substrates, but the tree was not affected because the lichen grew on dead bark. Today, scientists consider the relationship protocooperative: both entities benefit, but can exist without interacting. What is the benefit to the trees? Nutrients. Lichens get the majority of their nutrients out of the air, or through rain or fog. During rainy or foggy days, some of the lichens' nutrients become water soluble and fall around the tree's base. If the tree has a rich coating of lichens, the nutrients falling to the ground and being absorbed by the tree's roots act as liquid fertilizer. In fog-bathed coastal areas such as Mount Desert Island, prolific lichens, via this circuitous route, become an important source of nourishment for their host trees.

As you move farther down the boardwalk, red maple will begin to mix with gray and paper birch. Both these birches have white bark, but of the two species, only paper birch has bark that naturally peels off—sometimes in pieces the size of a sheet of paper, thus its common name.

The most northerly growing hardwood in eastern North America, paper birch has the greatest array of bark adaptations of any of our New England trees. It has four distinct bark features that allow it to grow at high latitudes. One is its white bark. This is distinctly different from our other regional trees, which have mostly brown or gray bark. Why would a tree whose range is centered in high latitudes have white bark? To reflect winter sunlight. On a still, cold, winter day during which the high temperature might only reach –10 degrees F, a tree with dark bark heats up during the few hours the sun skirts above the horizon. As the bark heats up it expands, as does the wood underneath it. Then, as the sun sets and the trunk rapidly cools, the bark contracts at a faster rate than the wood beneath it—causing the bark to split open in what is referred to as frost cracking. White bark resists that process.

Another distinct property of paper birch bark is its ability to peel. This is an adaptation to shed lichens and algae that would darken the bark and increase the risk of frost cracking.

▴ An array of crustose lichens grows on the trunk of a young red maple.

▴ This paper birch bark shows both peeling bark and areas darkened by gray-colored algae.

A close look at the bark on branches of a paper birch tree will show horizontal lines that are called lenticels. This is another special feature, as a tree with lenticels allows it to take carbon dioxide into its bark to conduct photosynthesis. If you gently scrape off the bark of a paper birch twig (or any tree with lenticels), you will see the color beneath the bark is green from the chlorophyll that resides there. Since paper birch reflects sunlight off its white bark, only the dark bark mostly found on branches does bark photosynthesis. Additionally, the water in the living cells of all New England trees does not freeze until –40 degrees F and remains liquid in a super-cooled state. If a paper birch tree's roots are not icebound and can take up water, it can do bark photosynthesis at temperatures below freezing, thus expanding its growing season.

The fourth unique quality of paper birch bark is that it is loaded with oils—so much so that it burns like kerosene. Paper birch survives temperatures lower than –40 degrees F by pumping its water outside of its cells, where it will freeze *between* the cells and not rupture them. However, when it gets that cold, the air is so dry that if the birch didn't seal itself in a vapor barrier of oil, its frozen moisture would be drawn out of the tree, desiccating and killing it. In this way, birch bark is like the original Gore-Tex waterproof fabric. Water can go into the lenticels, but it can't come out.

White bark to reflect winter sunlight and protect against frost cracking, peeling bark to keep it white and reflective, bark lenticels to expand the tree's growing season, and oily bark to prevent winter desiccation: all these advantages make paper birch bark the most highly evolved of all our New England trees.

At the end of the boardwalk, you can either walk straight back to the Sieur de Monts spring, turn left to head directly back to the parking lot, or venture onto one of the wonderful memorial paths to marvel at the stonework and spectacular views they offer.

GORHAM MOUNTAIN

Mount Desert Island summit hike and a sea cave

LOCATION ▸ Acadia National Park, Bar Harbor, Maine

FEATURES FOCUS ▸ Glacial impact, stump sprouts

DIFFICULTY
Moderate

LENGTH
2 miles

The hike up 525-foot Gorham Mountain is mostly on exposed, glacially scoured granite, some of which has been chiseled into stairs. There is a short section of irregular footing at the trail's start and more on the return, on Cadillac Cliffs Trail, so those who aren't sure-footed should take Gorham Mountain Trail all the way down. With expansive views of the ocean, Sand Beach, and the higher summits of Cadillac, Dorr, and Champlain Mountains commanding the eastern side of Mount Desert Island, this is a very popular hike and accessible any time of year.

Mount Desert Island is arguably the finest place in all of New England to see the erosional work of the Laurentide Ice Sheet, which covered a large portion of northern North America more than 20,000 years ago. This island is a textbook example of a glacially eroded landscape, with its numerous exposed ridgelines running north and south, each separated by a deep U-shaped valley. One of these valleys is Somes Sound, New England's only fjord. Hiking up Gorham Mountain, look for erosional features, particularly the exposed granite that was ground down for thousands of years by gla-

cial ice over a mile deep. In the 16,000 years since the glacier's departure, the rock has changed little—one reason granite is sometimes referred to as the rock of ages.

As you hike, the trail will be marked by Bates cairns. Waldron Bates was one of the early trail makers on Mount Desert Island in the late 19th and early 20th centuries. To mark his trails, Bates made stone structures (cairns) that were often composed of just four rocks: two base stones, a lintel that sat upon the

▲ A classic Bates cairn, pointing in the direction of the trail.

◄ Glacially scoured granite makes up a good portion of the Gorham Mountain ascent.

base stones, and a pointer stone that sat upon the lintel. Both the pointer stone and the gap between the base stones were aligned with the direction the trail was going. He was also the first trail maker on the island to build stairways out of granite—something that is now encountered on almost all Acadian trails—to make his paths easier to navigate.

Bates was very much intrigued by the geology of Mount Desert Island, building trails that would take hikers to unique natural features. Shortly after you begin hiking on the exposed granite, you will come to a plaque honoring Waldron Bates. The placement of the plaque at this location on the trail was purposeful; it occurs at a trail junction of Gorham Mountain Trail and Cadillac Cliffs Trail. Bates constructed Cadillac Cliffs Trail to take hikers along the base of sea stacks and a sea cave that are now almost 300 feet above the ocean's surface. How these geological features now reside high above the ocean that created them are discussed later in this chapter. At this point, continue on the Gorham Mountain Trail.

As you ascend, you will go through groves of pitch pine, scattered gray and paper birches, and striped maple. All these trees started growing following the Fire of 1947, which burned more than 17,000 acres on the east side of Mount Desert Island. They are small in stature for trees more than 70 years of age, because growth is slow in the thin, dry soils that top the granite. If you keep an eye peeled, you may see old cut stumps and the downed trunks of conifers that were killed by the fire. After the blaze, the standing snags were a bitter reminder of the destruction that had been wrought on the island. J. D. Rockefeller Jr. hired crews to cut down all the dead trees and their remains are still visible more than seven decades later.

About halfway up, you will begin getting good views out over the ocean from Sand Beach to Otter Point and beyond, to the islands that lie to the south and east of Mount Desert. The view of Sand Beach from Gorham Mountain is stunning. Interestingly, Sand Beach is not composed of sand at all, but of small fragments of clam and other shells that appear as sand unless closely examined with a hand lens.

Climbing higher, notice the trees become sparse and black huckleberry becomes more common. Huckleberry and its close relative, lowbush blueberry, are quite adapted to fire, so the big one of 1947 generated dense populations of these two shrubs. A major adaptation that they both share is heat-resistant roots. Lowbush blueberry roots can withstand temperatures of 1000 degrees F for up to 20 seconds. Fire will destroy all aboveground parts of these shrubs but not their roots. Just as important, fire will outright kill other shrubs that would compete with these two members of the heath family. After a blaze,

▲ Sand Beach, with Great Head to its right. In the far background is Schoodic Peninsula.

▲ The young, red, bell-shaped blossoms of black huckleberry, before it forms fruit.

blueberry and huckleberry roots sprout new aboveground growth and expand the size of the clones. In this way, fire is their friend. There are two great times to hike Gorham Mountain—in July, when the blueberry and huckleberry bushes have ripe fruit, and in mid-October, when the foliage of the black huckleberry turns crimson and these granite outcrop communities blaze as bright as any fire.

As you approach the summit, you will get some good views of the Beehive—one of Acadia National Park's most-climbed mountains. The Beehive is named for its shape as seen from Sand Beach. It resembles an old woven basket used to house bees. As seen from Gorham, its shape is that of a *roche moutonnée*: a bedrock outcropping shaped by an advancing glacier. The glacier ground down the north-facing slope of outcrops on Mount Desert Island into a low profile. However, as the sheet of ice passed over the outcropping, it latched onto the bedrock and quarried a steep south-facing side. The profiles of these structures were similar to the top and front of white wigs worn by men in the 18th century that were named "moutonnées." Since *roche* means "stone" in French, the translation for roche moutonnée is "stone wig." The Beehive is the largest roche moutonnée on Mount Desert Island.

Reaching the summit you will have a fine view of Cadillac and Dorr Mountains to the northwest. Everything in this view from the Gorham Mountain peak was burned in the 1947 fire, generating miles-long ridgeline hikes with expansive views that are magnets for hikers. Also at the summit you will see scattered pitch pines,

‣ From this angle, the Beehive has a gentle, north-facing slope on the left and a steep, quarried side on the right.

many of them coppiced, with a number of trunks growing from their root system. Pitch pine is our only regional conifer that can stump sprout—an adaptation to fire or cutting. This allowed pitch pines to survive the 1947 fire.

On the way down, you will come to the upper junction of Cadillac Cliffs Trail. It's a more challenging trail in terms of footing and steepness, so if the hike up Gorham was as ambitious as you feel comfortable tackling, continue down the Gorham Mountain Trail. For those who are confident on a steeper, more irregular trail, Cadillac Cliffs Trail is worth the effort. The start of the upper end of the trail is a steep descent to a sea cave, which is accessed at the bottom by crossing a short wooden bridge. As you gaze into the cave, you'll notice that it has a low ceiling but extends a fair distance back. Take note of the rounded boulders stuck within the cave. These are ocean cobbles pushed into the cave by wave action some 17,000 years ago. As you continue on the trail past this sea cave, you will come to sea stacks, vertical landforms that form near coastlines. Here, the stacks are made of granite and have been rounded by wave action. The

‣ from top Cadillac and Dorr Mountains can be seen from the summit of Gorham Mountain.
‣ A coppiced pitch pine that survived the 1947 fire.

question is, if the cave and sea stacks were generated by waves, how can they now be almost 300 feet above the ocean?

Before the Laurentide Ice Sheet started to recede around 17,000 years ago, ice more than a mile thick lay upon Mount Desert Island. The massive weight of that ice pushed the continental crust in the region hundreds of feet down into the malleable mantle of the Earth. After the glacier was gone, the level of the ocean in relationship to the land was almost 300 feet higher than it is today, creating the sea cave and sea stacks. With the removal of all that ice weight, the continental crust started to slowly rise out of the denser mantle, not unlike a freighter that gets unloaded rises up out of the water. After thousands of years of what is called isostatic rebounding, these features that were once at sea level now lie almost 300 feet above the ocean.

On your way down to the lower portion of Cadillac Cliffs Trail, you will go through a small boulder cave as well as some narrow aisles where the trail is lined by walls of granite on each side. This trail placement was intentionally chosen by Bates to delight avid hikers. When you join up with the Gorham Mountain Trail, go left to return to the parking lot.

▸ clockwise from top left This rounded cobble boulder jammed into the Gorham Mountain sea cave was delivered by wave action 17 millennia ago. ▪ A granite sea stack rounded by wave action is now more than 300 feet above sea level. ▪ The entrance of the Gorham Mountain sea cave, along the Cadillac Cliffs Trail.

ORONO BOG

Pillows and cradles and carnivorous plants

DIFFICULTY
Easy

LENGTH
1.25 miles

LOCATION ▸ Bangor, Maine
FEATURES FOCUS ▸ Glacial impact, pillows and cradles, white pine weevil

This is a level trail with a boardwalk loop into the Orono Bog. During rainy periods, the short trail leading to the boardwalk may have wet patches. A great time to do this exploration is in mid- to late June, when blooms are at their peak.

The Orono Bog differs from Saco Heath in a couple of ways. The peat development in the Saco Heath is more compact for one thing, creating a more stable substrate. This allows Saco Heath to support large trees, such as mature pitch pines, as well as a very dense shrub layer dominated by leatherleaf. The Orono Bog has trees, but of much smaller stature, and Orono's shrub layer is not as dense, giving rise to a greater diversity of plant species. Another difference between the two areas is that the University of Maine has developed excellent interpretive signs along the boardwalk at Orono Bog. In fact, I think it may be the finest interpreted trail I have ever experienced.

To get to the boardwalk that loops through the bog, walk a quarter mile from the parking area on a level trail that passes through three different wooded communities. Starting the trail, you will be in a forest of weevil-hit white pines. These pines colonized a pasture that was abandoned to grow back to forest around 1990. White pines produce one tier of limbs each year, which grows around the trunk at a particular height. Each tier is known as a limb whorl. By counting the number of limb whorls from the base of the tree to its top, one can determine the age of a white pine. When I made my site visit in 2019, I counted 30 limb whorls on a number of these pines to determine when the pasture was abandoned.

Trees hit by the white pine weevil have their trunks split into at least two new trunks. The top shoot of a pine is killed, and limbs in the whorl immediately below the top shoot grow upward to create the replacement trunks. In a dense stand of weevil-impacted white pines such as this one, trees only send up two of their limbs to become new trunks.

A close look at the surface of the ground in this pine stand will show that it is lumpy. The lumps are the pits and mounds, called pillows and cradles, created when live trees are uprooted by either strong winds or snow- and ice-loading events. When a live tree falls, its root mass rips out of the ground (tip-up), creating a pit or cradle. The upturned roots then slowly decay, redepositing the soil they brought up from the pit, forming a mound or pillow. Large pillows and cradles can be visible up to 1000 years after a live tree has fallen. Given the robust disturbance regime in New England—frequent thunderstorm microbursts, occasional hurricanes and nor'easters, and wet snow and ice storms—it's not surprising that after a few centuries, many woodland forest floors in this region are carpeted with pillows and cradles. When hay and other crop fields were created in the 19th century, they were plowed to remove these pits and mounds. Sites that were solely used as pasture were not plowed, and retained their bumps and cavities. Their presence con-firms that this site was once a pasture that became abandoned and was then colonized by white pine. As you move deeper into the for-est, the white pines are replaced by older red oaks, which indicates that this section of the forest was abandoned earlier than the white pine portion. At that time, the oaks were producing a lot of acorns and white pines were not producing seeds.

Both the red oak and white pine are masting species. This means that they do not produce seeds every year, but rather coordinate with other members of their species to produce a huge crop of seeds every few years. The trees communicate via aerosol chemicals to determine the mast (seeding) years. During the years when seeds are not pro-duced, trees store the energy they have saved as starch in their roots. Two, three, four, five, or maybe six years later, they all mobilize that energy and come forth with a mast year. Walking in an oak-dominated woodland during a mast year is like walking on a surface covered in marbles. This means that red oak and white pine stands exist in cohorts of individual trees that are all the same age.

The reason trees mast is to thwart seed consumers. For red oaks, the major consumer of acorns is the acorn weevil. During the month

◂ The start of the swamp portion of the boardwalk at Orono Bog.

of July, the females of this small insect species lay an egg in every acorn they can find. When the acorn weevil larvae emerge, they start eating the meat of the acorn, reducing its viability. If all the oaks in a region can suppress acorn production for a number of years in a row, they dramatically depress the acorn weevil population—then overwhelm them during a mast year. This is so successful for red oaks that if you see an oak in the tree canopy, you can be very sure it was spawned during a mast year.

After passing through the red oak woodland, you will enter a swamp dominated by balsam fir, identified by the rounded bumps on its smooth bark. Those bumps are resin blisters filled with sticky pitch, which protect balsam firs from insects like bark beetles. When a beetle enters a resin blister, it becomes trapped in the pitch. The presence of the balsam fir swamp indicates that you are getting close to the boardwalk. Just before you reach the walkway, on the left side of the trail, is a very large weevil-hit white pine that is probably at least 150 years of age.

As you start on the boardwalk you will be in a tree swamp dominated by red maple with scattered black ash, and an understory composed of speckled alder and winterberry holly. Black ash is also known as basket ash because it is the species used by the Wabanaki First Nations for making baskets. Another species worth noting in this swamp sports a basal rosette of large green leaves. This is skunk cabbage, named for the odor given off by its leaves when broken.

Skunk cabbage is one of our earliest flowering plants, often blooming before the snow has completely melted away. In early spring its flowers come out of the ground as a reddish spathe lined in green. Its appearance is meant to be similar to rotting flesh, as is its smell. This is to attract carrion flies and beetles looking for dead carcasses on which to lay their eggs. When the flies land on the skunk cabbage, they pollinate its flowers—an important deception for the cabbage, as there are not many other active pollinators in early spring. Because the skunk cabbage benefits by being pollinated, while the insects seem to get nothing in return, the plant could be considered to be parasitizing the insects. However, the flowers of the skunk cabbage are also thermogenic, meaning they produce heat to melt surrounding snow and possibly make the spathe warm and more attractive to insects. Because the insects are able to warm themselves on the skunk cabbage's spathe, perhaps this is actually a relationship in which both parties benefit.

Continuing down the boardwalk, the acidity of the swamp will increase and black spruce and larch will begin to prevail. Skunk cabbage will still be present, demonstrating that it has a wide pH tolerance range. Just before you reach the bog, the boardwalk will cut across a small island composed of glacial till—a jumble of material dropped in place by melting glacial ice—as can be seen by its surficial (formed on the surface) rocks. When you reach the open bog portion of the boardwalk, bear right.

As mentioned previously, the trees in the Orono Bog are much smaller in stature than those in Saco Heath. However, don't let their size deceive you regarding their age. Many of the black spruce that are only slightly taller than a person are upwards of 100 years old. This can be confirmed by counting their limb whorls, which are tightly stacked one above another.

A good time to visit Orono Bog is in late June when its grass pink and pitcher plants are in bloom and quite common all along the board-walk. The grass pink is an orchid. Its presence and that of members of the heath family—such as highbush blueberry, sheep laurel, leather-leaf, rhodora, and bog rosemary—mean that there are mycorrhizal fungi present in the bog. Mycorrhizae are fungi that associate with the roots of plants to get their carbohydrate energy. These fungi are not parasites, because any plant that associates with them can dramatically increase its nutrient uptake via the mycorrhizal network—critically important in a bog were the high acidity leaches nutrients away. Many groups of plants, including heaths and orchids,

▲ The basal rosette of a skunk cabbage features large green leaves.

▲ The beginning of the bog portion of the boardwalk.

▲ A section of a black spruce with more than 30 tightly stacked limb whorls.

▲ Hummocks with small trees and taller shrubs, in contrast to the foreground, which is a quaking mat.

▲ A low hummock with a few small larch trees supports orange sphagnum, while on each side of the hummock is a darker red species of sphagnum.

are so highly coevolved with mycorrhizae that they have to associate with them to survive.

Moving farther into the bog you will notice hummocks—raised portions of the bog that are a bit more stable—supporting black spruce, larch, and taller heaths, while the lower portions of the bog have shrubs of much shorter height. This is because the lower areas are less stable and quake more. A close look at the sphagnum moss of the quaking portions versus that on the hummocks shows they are different species. The so-called quaking sphagnums are a deeper red and those on the hummocks are more orange.

Looking closely at the black spruce growing on the hummocks, note that the spruce in the center is often taller than those growing around it. In fact, most of the spruce trees on a hummock are often just one individual creating a tree candelabra. When a low branch of a spruce makes contact with the sphagnum of a hummock, it can take root and then send up a new trunk from that branch. A limb rooting like this is called layering and it happens in many species of conifers, creating a cluster of trunks whose arrangement is reminiscent of a candelabra, thus the name of these tree clones.

Off in the distance you will see taller black spruce and larch bordering the bog. These are areas where the peat deposition is solid enough to support large trees, as the bog succeeds to an acidic tree swamp similar to the one the boardwalk went through.

Before heading back into the tree swamp on the boardwalk, take a few minutes to examine the pitcher plants, an unusual group of plants that are carnivorous, or insect eating. The so-called pitchers are the plant's leaves, and they have an unusual but essential purpose. Nutrients are extremely limited in the bog, so the pitcher plant consumes insects—not for their energy, but for the nutrients encased in their bodies (hence the carnivorous designation). To accomplish this, each pitcher has a slippery overhanging lip. When insects land on this lip, they slip into the pitcher and the leaf's stiff, downward-pointing hairs keep the insects from climbing back out. Eventually, the bugs become exhausted and fall into a pool of liquid at the bottom of the pitcher, where they drown. Their nutrients are slowly leached out and absorbed by the plant. Since the carcasses of some insects don't completely decompose, there are also invertebrates that live in pitcher plants and eat the carcasses of the dead insects. When they excrete the insect's remains, the plant can absorb even more nutrients. This is another mutually beneficial interaction between species—here, the pitcher plant and its resident invertebrate.

When you come to the end of the boardwalk loop, you can choose to return to the parking area, do the boardwalk loop again, or possibly explore another trail in this unique city park.

▲ A black spruce tree candelabra.

▲ In the distance, taller spruce and larch can be seen in the acidic tree swamp bordering the bog.

▲ The insect-consuming pitcher plant in flower.

MOUNT AGAMENTICUS

Clues to early New England; a panoramic reward

DIFFICULTY
Moderate

LENGTH
2.25 miles

LOCATION ▸ York, Maine

FEATURES FOCUS ▸ Tree secrets: black birch, glacial impact, pillows and cradles, stone walls and early agriculture, stump sprouts

This is a mostly level hike with two short sections that may be a bit more challenging: the short ascent on the Summit Staircase Trail and the descent on the Sweet Fern Trail. The ascent includes a section of jumbled boulders; if you feel you will not be comfortable on them, continue past the Summit Staircase Trail and turn right on the road back to the summit parking lot. The descent section is fine during dry times, but if the granite is wet it will be slick.

Mount Agamenticus stands at 692 feet, just 5 miles from the Atlantic Ocean and 10 miles north of Maine's southern boundary. Its placement is significant for two important reasons. In 1497 it was spotted by Italian navigator John Cabot, making it the first recorded land sighting in what is now New England by a 15th-century European explorer. The peak's other claim to fame is that geographically it lies at both the northern and southern range limits of a number of species, such as chestnut oak (northern limit) and red spruce (southern limit), making it the most species-rich regional ecosystem in all of Maine.

The exploration starts at the summit on the Big A Trail, which shortly leads to the Fisher Trail on the right. Take the Fisher Trail a short distance down, until you come back to a lower portion of the Big A Trail. At this junction, turn right on Big A. You will pass through early successional vegetation that is managed for summit views and for early successional species. When you reach the intersection with the Vulture's View Trail, there will be an outcropping of granite on the right with a stand of eastern hemlock growing out of

its crevices. What is striking about this outcrop community is that there is no soil, just granite and hemlock trees! I have witnessed communities like this on granite outcrops in Yosemite National Park, but not in New England. What makes it even more striking is that it is hemlock, not the pitch pine that is usually found growing on New England granite.

A stand of hemlock grows out of an exposed granite ledge.

This granite outcrop is a clue to Mount Agamenticus's existence. The mountain is technically a monadnock—a geological term borrowed from a word in the Abenaki language that means "mountain that stands alone." The erosion-resistant granite has allowed Agamenticus to persist while other surrounding features have been eroded down. Continue on the Big A Trail, you will soon come to a junction with the Sweet Fern Trail at an abandoned ski-lift tower. Turn left on Sweet Fern and as you descend, the tread of the trail will be glacially scoured granite—the tough bedrock that has allowed this mountain to persist. The trail also follows one of the mountain's former ski slopes, abandoned in 1974.

On the descent, both sides of the exposed trail are carpeted in extensive mats of moss growing right on the scoured granite. The moss first established in crevices in the granite, then expanded up and out of the crevices to sprawl across the bedrock. The moss eventually thickened to a point that allowed herbaceous plants such as grasses and goldenrods to establish, followed by mats of bearberry; checkerberry, with its wintergreen-scented leaves; and trailing arbutus, whose April blossoms are as fragrant as honeysuckle. In time, trees such as red oak established, allowing forests to develop on the

granite. Farther along, where seeps run over the granite, you may notice sphagnum moss mixed in with hair cap moss, which is the predominant moss in these mats. Hair cap is so named because in summer it produces spore capsules that are covered by small, hairy caps that can be carefully pulled off.

When you reach the third ski-lift tower from the junction of the Big A Trail, the exposed granite will display clear glacial striations—straight, parallel gouges etched into the granite—which formed as the small rocks (often quartz) that were embedded in the glacial ice scraped over the bedrock. You may also notice crescentic gouges—a series of crescent-shaped fractures in the bedrock—created by a boulder at the bottom of the glacier repeatedly striking the granite. With each hit, a small crescent-shaped flake of granite was removed. These two features are charac-

⁺ from top An extensive mat of moss covers the glacially scoured granite. • A sphagnum moss colony emerges from a carpet of hair cap moss.

teristic of north-facing slopes of regional granite where the glacier, as it flowed upslope, slowly abraded the granite. South-facing slopes often experienced far greater erosion through glacial plucking or quarrying. This occurred as the glacier latched onto the bedrock, pulled chunks off, then carried them away as large boulders. Thus, south-facing slopes of our regional bedrock hills and summits often display steep, jagged slopes such as the Beehive, a feature of the Gorham Mountain hike, also in Maine.

Soon you will come to the junction with the Ring Trail. Here, look back up the Sweet Fern Trail and you may see the granite's shining glacial polish if the lighting is right. This section of granite was polished smooth by fine silt and sand in the glacial ice that was dragged across the bedrock under great pressure. Turn right on the Ring Trail and you will soon be at a four-way intersection. Keep heading straight onto the Chestnut Oak Trail and enter a section of forest that was never cleared and therefore hosts many older trees. This woodland is not old growth because there is clear evidence of logging, but it does hold black birch trees that are likely two centuries old, judging by their bark.

▲ Straight, parallel, striations can be seen on glacially scoured granite.

Black birch bark texture changes as it ages, starting with smooth, black bark, then developing vertical fissures. Around 80 years, the bark creates rectangular-shaped plates. At a century and a half, the plates drop, revealing smooth bark once again, without lenticels. Nearing 200 years, the bark establishes vertical ridges. At the beginning of the Chestnut Oak Trail, keep an eye out for a black birch on the left side of the trail that is

▲ Glacially polished granite shines like ice at the bottom of the Sweet Fern Trail.

only about one foot in diameter but has vertical bark ridges, indicating it is at least 200 years old. You can also see a photo of what old black birch bark looks like in the chapter on Pisgah State Park in New Hampshire.

As you continue down the Chestnut Oak Trail, you will see specimens of the trail's namesake tree species, identified by their thick

This chestnut oak has characteristic coarse bark ridges and deep fissures.

This coppiced chestnut oak has multiple trunks as a result of logging.

Downy rattlesnake plantain sends up a spike of tiny orchid blossoms.

bark ridges and deep fissures. Chestnut oak grows in dry, nutrient-poor soils and finds its northeastern range limits here in York County, Maine. When in leaf, this species can be identified by its unlobed leaves with margins that support many rounded teeth, making it somewhat resemble the leaves of American chestnut.

Many of the chestnut oaks you encounter will be coppiced, supporting two, three, or even four trunks. This is evidence of past logging events, when trees were cut and they subsequently stump sprouted. It appears that some of these coppiced trees were cut over 100 years ago, and based on the size of their original trunks, were probably over 100 years old when cut. This would make their root systems around two centuries old. Because the existing trunks sprouted from the base of the original tree, the size of their original trunks can be estimated by drawing a circle at ground level through the centers of their existing trunks.

Along the Chestnut Oak Trail, look for a small herbaceous plant whose evergreen leaves are checkered with white veins. This is the downy rattlesnake plantain, an uncommon native orchid. As long as there is no snow cover, this plant will be visible. As an orchid it has to interact with mycorrhizae—fungi that associate with the roots of photosynthetic plants and extract sugars from those plants. It may sound like the fungi are parasitizing their host plants, but it is actually a mutually beneficial relationship. This is because plants that associate with mycorrhizae can dramatically increase nutrient and water uptake. In fact, this is such an important relationship, many of our native plants cannot exist without a mycorrhizal partner—including most of our coniferous trees; all the members of our heath family (such as blueberry, bearberry, and checkerberry); and, like the downy rattlesnake plantain, all members of the orchid family.

When in bloom, downy rattlesnake plantain produces a spike—a stalk supporting flowers that do not have stems for attachment. Such blooms are called sessile.

The "downy" in this plant's name is derived from the fine coat of hairs that covers the spike. After being pollinated by local bees, the flowers form capsules holding very tiny seeds. Plants with such seed capsules on a stiff stalk have a very specific form of seed dispersal: catapulting. Animals that accidentally bend the stalk back and then release it get showered with hundreds of small seeds. These seeds are then carried away and dispersed widely.

Just before reaching the junction with the Porcupine Trail, you may see a downed tree on the right that seems to have popped out of the ground. Its roots decayed into round knobs that could no longer anchor the tree. This was an oak killed by repeated gypsy moth defoliations back in the early 1980s. The dead snags of these oaks stood for about 25 years and then, like this one, eventually just fell over. This is classic for oak snags. Most other species don't uproot, but break off from their stump a couple of feet above ground.

Turn right at the junction onto the Porcupine Trail. You will see a stone fence on the right. Looking at the surficial topography on both sides of this fence, you may notice a difference: the ground on the right side of the fence is smooth on the surface while the ground on the left looks lumpy. The lumpy terrain on the left is the result of pits and mounds, or pillow and cradle topography. Pillows and cradles are the result of trees uprooting, leaving a root crater (cradle), then as roots decay over time, dropping soil adjacent to the crater (pillow). When pillows and cradles are not present, as on the right side of the fence, they have been removed by agricultural plowing.

The farmers who grew hay only plowed a few times, to remove the pillows and cradles and smooth the ground for scything. Hay's perennial roots then prevented rocks from slowly moving to the surface during freeze-thaw cycles. Fields with crops had no perennial root systems, and long-buried rocks began moving vertically in the freezes and thaws of the seasons. These crop fields started producing lots of rocks, many the size of a fist, that needed to be removed for planting—but found homes in bordering stone fences.

So: stone fences in the area without fist-sized rocks that have adjacent smooth topography suggest that the fence was once adjacent to a hayfield. Stone fences that contain small rocks are a clue that other, non-perennial crops were grown there.

▲ It's best to leave a colony of Allegheny mound ants to themselves.

▲ An extensive mat of bearberry thrives near the summit of Mount Agamenticus.

▲ The Atlantic Ocean is visible in the distance from the summit of Mount Agamenticus.

A close look at this stone wall reveals that there are no small rocks, indicating the smooth, even ground is a former hayfield.

Where the Porcupine Trail joins the Rocky Road Trail, look for some large mounds. These are the homes of Allegheny mound ants, which can number up to 100,000 individuals per colony. Mounds are often 3–9 feet in diameter and many feet in height. They usually are free of surrounding ground vegetation, up to a 50-foot radius around the mound. The ants kill the surrounding vegetation by poisoning it with formic acid. They are foragers that eat both plants and animals. Be careful not to antagonize these small but formidable characters or they will attack with painful stings.

At the junction of the Rocky Road Trail and the Ring Trail, continue straight across this four-way intersection and eventually turn right onto the Summit Staircase Trail. Be sure to follow the red blazes on the rock of the Summit Staircase. Leaving the forest, you will encounter large mats of bearberry, a heath that is quite spotty in New England. In fact, this is only the third place in the region that I've encountered bearberry. The other two are in Acadia National Park on Mount Desert Island and in the Cape Cod National Seashore. However, neither of those places has a mat of bearberry as extensive as found here, approaching the summit of Mount Agamenticus.

Finally, at the top of the Summit Staircase Trail, you will be rewarded with an extensive view out to the Atlantic Ocean. At this location, you are 5 miles east of the spot where John Cabot landed and explored over five centuries ago. As you take in the coastline, also keep in mind that these are waters the Abenaki First Nation canoed for thousands of years before Cabot's arrival.

GREAT WASS ISLAND PRESERVE

Open-in-case-of-fire pine cones and a granite beach

DIFFICULTY
Difficult

LOCATION ▸ Beals, Maine
FEATURES FOCUS ▸ Glacial impact

LENGTH
4 miles

Although this trail is fairly level, without any long climbs or descents, the hike may be challenging for some because of sections of irregular footing and its round-trip length. It is also a very wild trail that doesn't get a lot of visitors. The payoff is substantial, though, in that that it leads to an absolutely pristine and gorgeous section of the Bold Coast of Maine.

Like the Saco Heath, Great Wass Island Preserve is another gem that has been protected by The Nature Conservancy. It is also the most remote and wild exploration covered in this book.

To get to the trailhead, travel south from Jonesport on Bridge Street, across the bridge to Beals; turn left onto Bay View Drive and follow for a mile. Just beyond the causeway to Great Wass Island, at the intersection, turn right onto Black Duck Cove Road and continue 2 miles to reach the trailhead parking lot on the left side of the road.

About 100 yards down the trail, there is a fork. Take the right hand fork onto the Little Cape Point Trail and begin your exploration of this boreal forest dominated by spruce, balsam fir, paper birch, and American mountain ash. The latter tree is not actually an ash, but rather a member of the rose family. In 2019 it had a bumper crop of berries throughout northern New England, with branches bent down under the weight of huge clusters of bright red fruit. I was once at high elevation in the White Mountains of New Hampshire on a very cold January day, during a similarly heavy fruiting year for mountain ash. A huge flock of eastern bluebirds were foraging on the berries at 3500 feet. I later inquired about this with an ornithologist friend, who answered that during abundant fruit years, bluebirds overwinter at high elevations because these berries are such a great energy resource.

Like so many of Down East Maine's coastal forests, this one is carpeted in beds of moss and reindeer lichen, which benefit from the frequent fog that shrouds this maritime environment. Such mats of moss and lichen are called cryptogamic, which means hidden seeds (they reproduce by spores), and add a rich dimension to the understories of boreal (northern conifer) forests. I often marvel at the various textures in these mats; they remind me of flying over a mixed conifer and hardwood forest in November—the reindeer lichen look like leafless hardwood trees. Along with these are alpine species that usually occur above the tree line in New England, but here are

◄ Beds of moss carpet the understory.

found growing at sea level because of the windy, cool, moist weather. Such conditions are spawned by the cold waters brought south by the Labrador Current in this part of the Gulf of Maine. The Labrador Current flows south into the North Atlantic Ocean from the Arctic Ocean, hugging the coast of Labrador, passing Newfoundland and the east coast of Canada, and carrying a cold flow from Maine to Massachusetts. Cool-loving species here include black crowberry, with its tiny leaves that make it appear more like a moss, and mountain cranberry with its waxy, evergreen leaves.

After crossing an ephemeral stream, you will encounter a section of boardwalk over a bed of sphagnum moss. Then you will enter one of the largest stands of jack pine in New England. Jack pine is identified by its short needles, which make it appear more like a spruce than a pine. Unlike white pine, with its clusters of five needles, or pitch pine with clusters of three, jack pine needles grow in pairs. This is North America's most northerly growing pine, and the short needles are an adaptation to reduce surface area and avoid desiccation on cold winter nights. It is also a tree that often has an irregular, almost unruly growth form.

Jack pine is also ingeniously adapted to fire. It has serotinous cones, which stay closed and hold viable seeds up to 25 years. These cones only open when the temperature around them climbs above

◂ This stand of jack pine shows the trees' irregular growth form.

▲ The closed, gray serotinous cones of a jack pine hold seeds only released during fire.

▲ The trail, as it runs over a granite outcropping, is surrounded by jack pine.

125 degrees F—in other words, as the result of a fire. Jack pine's small seeds cannot establish in a normal bed of forest litter; they need the bare soil created by fire. If the fire is a surface type, it will take the serotinous cones up to 12 hours to open, releasing the seeds after the fire is out. However, if it is a crown fire (traveling through the tree-tops) and the temperature around the cones gets extremely hot, the cones will open in a matter of minutes, releasing the seeds into the blaze. Luckily, jack pine seeds can withstand temperatures up to 700 degrees F for about 15 seconds. In a crown fire there are very strong updrafts, and the seeds are lifted up and far away from the blaze, hopefully to land in an area where the fire has burned out. Jack pine also has regular cones that open when mature, but its percentage of serotinous cones is greater than in any other species of tree. To find serotinous cones, look for closed, curved, gray cones a number of twig whorls down from a branch tip.

Despite its complex system for preserving seeds during fire, the jack pine tree itself is surprisingly vulnerable to blazes. With relatively thin bark and no ability to stump sprout, jack pines will die in a wild-fire. But I often think of this species as being the phoenix of trees—it dies in a dramatic blaze only to arise from the ashes by way of its carefully protected seeds.

Throughout the jack pine community are glacially exposed areas of granite bedrock that the trail crosses, making for easy walking. Adjacent to the tread of the trail in these areas, the granite will be covered by crustose and foliose lichens. Crustose lichens are the simplest in form, looking like they have simply been painted on the bedrock. Because the entire crustose lichen is welded onto the bedrock, it is very hard to remove. Common species on Great Wass's granite are gray cinder lichen and green map lichen.

If you think about it, colonizing on an exposed granite outcrop requires organisms to deal with an array of challenges. With no soil, how do plants anchor themselves and get nutrients? On sunny days when the granite is completely dry, how does vegetation obtain necessary moisture? Because crustose lichens are the only group that can handle these challenges, they are the pioneer community or first species to establish on granite. For anchoring, they have thousands of minute fungal threads called rhyzines that grow into the bedrock, bonding the lichen to the stone. For sustenance, crustose lichens gather most of their nutrients from the air or from fog or rainwater. To deal with desiccation they are cryptobiotic, which means when the moisture levels in their tissues drops to about 10 percent, they enter a complete dormancy in which no chemical reactions occur. Some lichens can exist in this state for up to a century, then, in a rare fog or rainfall, quickly resume all metabolic activities.

After a number of decades, crustose lichens will cover the granite. By this time, there is a thin veneer of nutrients in the lichens and they can hold moisture for a longer period than bare granite can. This allows the next community to establish: the foliose lichens. Unlike crustose lichens, foliose lichens are not completely attached to the bedrock and look more like leaves. The most common foliose lichen growing on this island's granite is target lichen—a light green type that sometimes grows in a series of concentric rings, accounting for its name. More commonly, it grows in a mazelike pattern.

You can walk on crustose lichens, because they are so securely anchored to the bedrock, but foot traffic will kill foliose lichens. Because it can take up to 50 years to create a viable covering of target lichen and one footstep can eradicate it in mere seconds, it's important to make every effort to not step on these fragile organisms.

When lichens in the cryptobiotic phase are stepped on, you will hear a crunching sound as they are crushed. To protect these wonderful lichen communities on the granite of Great Wass Island, and keep them in good shape, please be sure to stay in the middle of the trail when crossing granite outcrops.

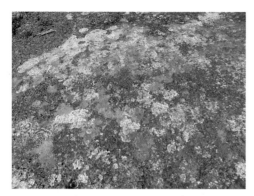

▲ Lichen-encrusted granite is populated with cinder, green map, and target lichens.

▲ An alpine reindeer lichen colony exists around a young lowbush blueberry.

▲ Black spruce can be identified by their living topknots and slim trunks of dead branches below.

In crevices or depressions on the granite, you will often find moss and reindeer lichen communities. My favorite lichen is alpine reindeer lichen, with its tight clusters that resemble a head of cauliflower. These are also very fragile and should never be stepped on; however, on rainy or foggy days, be sure to bend over and gently feel how spongy they are when not in their cryptobiotic state.

Mixed in with the jack pine is also black spruce—a tree that in New England is usually only found in bogs or the alpine zones of our highest peaks. Here, similar to the black crowberry and mountain cranberry, black spruce grows as a member of the forest community, just as it does hundreds of miles north in the boreal forests of Canada and Alaska. Black spruce is easily recognized by it growth form: a very narrow tree with a topknot of live branches, below which are mostly dead branches. I am not sure why black spruce grows like this, but it is a common feature of the species. Many black spruce are draped in green usnea lichen, commonly known as old man's beard, a result of the island's frequent fogs. Usnea is very sensitive to air pollution and its presence tells us that the air quality here is good.

Continuing down the trail, you will alternate between glacially shaped granite outcrop communities and spruce forest. Eventually you will come to a small bog crossed via boardwalk. This bog holds dense clusters of pitcher plants right along the boardwalk for very

▴ An elegant cluster of pitcher plants, waiting patiently for their insect prey.

▴ Root systems of spruce trees killed by high tides due to climate change.

The end of the trail is the beautiful granite shore of Great Wass Island. ▸

close viewing. Pitcher plants are carnivorous plants that attract and trap insects by way of a slippery leaf called a pitcher. After sliding down the leaf into a small pool, insects drown and their nutrients are absorbed into the plant.

After the bog, the environment will continue to alternate between jack pine and spruce forest communities until you reach the ocean, with its graceful granite shoreline. Looking to your left after emerging from the forest, you will see the root systems of spruce trees that once grew close to the high-tide line. Due to sea level rise and the ensuing frequent high tides, those trees are now dead—a consequence of climate change, and an indication of things to come.

After exploring the shoreline, you can return on the Little Cape Point Trail. If you are up for a bit longer exploration, you can follow the shoreline to the left, past the drowned spruce trees, and around Little Cape Point, then on to the Mud Hole Trail. It will take you back to the parking lot. That entire loop is 5.5 miles, versus the 4-mile round trip on the Little Cape Point Trail.

NEW HAMPSHIRE

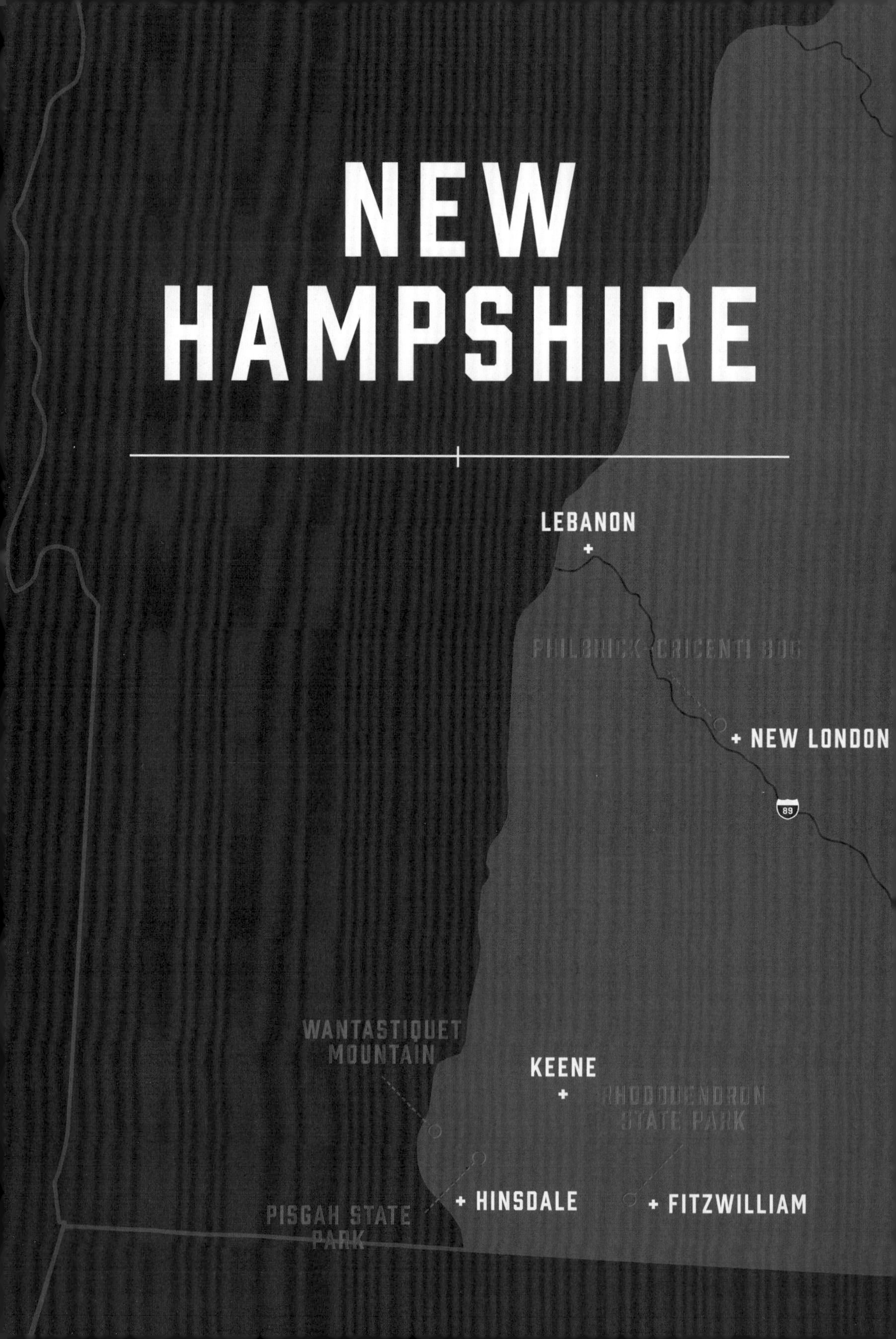

LEBANON
+

PHILBRICK-CRICENTI BOG

+ NEW LONDON

[89]

WANTASTIQUET
MOUNTAIN

KEENE
+

RHODODENDRON
STATE PARK

PISGAH STATE
PARK

+ HINSDALE

+ FITZWILLIAM

Mt. Washington Auto Road
+

LILAC GARDEN

Crawford Notch
State Park
+

WHITE
MOUNTAIN
NATIONAL
FOREST

DRY RIVER OLD GROWTH

+ BARTLETT

+ CONCORD
MANCHESTER
CEDAR SWAMP

+ MANCHESTER
293

93

AREA OF DETAIL

ALPINE GARDEN

A celebrated road plus high-elevation marvels

DIFFICULTY
Moderate

LOCATION ‣ White Mountain National Forest, New Hampshire
FEATURES FOCUS ‣ Glacial impact

LENGTH
2 miles

This may be the most fiscally extravagant exploration covered in this book: on a recent trip, the fee to drive up the famous Mount Washington Auto Road was $35. The 7.6-mile Auto Road was first opened to the public in 1861 and claims to be the oldest continuously operating attraction in the country. It is also the first leg of this adventure.

After the brief road trip, the hike is a couple miles out and back, with some irregular terrain. The excursion can be shortened by hiking down Huntington Ravine Trail to access Alpine Garden Trail; however, this shortcut should only be attempted by sure-footed hikers as the upper portion of Huntington Ravine Trail is a steep jumble of boulders. The best time to visit the Alpine Garden is in mid-June, when most everything is in bloom.

Mount Washington's Alpine Garden is considered to be the finest and most plant-diverse example of alpine tundra in the northeastern United States. During a good bloom year, walking along the Alpine Garden Trail in the third week of June is similar to strolling through a beautifully maintained rock garden with carpets of pink and white flowers. However, unlike most rock gardens, it has the bonus of dramatic mountain views.

The Alpine Garden is located on a mile-high terrace on Mount Washington's eastern side, just above and lying between its two great, glacial cirques: Tuckerman and Huntington Ravines. A glacial cirque is a U-shaped valley gnawed into the side of a mountain by an alpine glacier. As snow builds up to a depth of about 200 feet, the great pressure transforms snow into ice. However, unlike the ice we are used to, this ice can slowly move. Being pulled by gravity, it flows downhill with strong erosive force, cutting back into the mountain's side and creating a bowl-shaped valley. The alpine glaciers that formed these ravines no longer exist, although snow can persist in Tuckerman Ravine almost through the entire year.

There are two trailheads to the Alpine Garden from the Auto Road as it climbs to the mountain's summit. One is off a small parking lot at the 6-mile post, about a tenth of a mile before the Alpine Garden Trail intersects the road. If that first lot is full, continue another mile up to a larger lot for the top of the Huntington Ravine Trail. The hike down the Huntington Ravine Trail to the

‹ Rock cairns line the Alpine Garden Trail, with Tuckerman Ravine in the distance.

Alpine Garden Trail is over irregular boulders, so should only be used by confident trekkers.

At the junction of the Alpine Garden and Huntington Ravine Trails, the Alpine Garden Trail stretches south toward Tuckerman Ravine. Its route through the garden can be seen snaking off in the distance, delineated by numerous tall stone cairns shaped like huge beehives. The closeness of these cairns to each other is indicative of the extreme weather conditions that frequent Mount Washington. Until 1996, when a hurricane near Australia spawned a wind gust of 253 miles an hour, Mount Washington held the record of the highest-speed gust ever recorded, with a 1934 wind burst of 231 miles an hour. Over 100 days a year, winds on the mountain exceed hurricane force, making it the one of the windiest places on earth. This is quite a striking feature considering the mountain is less than 6300 feet in height. Along with the winds come fogs and whiteout conditions that can reduce visibility to just a few yards—hence the close proximity of the cairns.

Walking down the Alpine Garden Trail, you will encounter a variety of high-altitude ecological communities strongly influenced by wind. On the most extreme sites, where winter winds remove all snow cover, you will encounter fellfields—alpine ecosystems dominated by exposed boulders surrounded by low-growing mats of alpine plants. Because of the harsh winds, plants in fellfields must hug the ground. Here, two June-blooming alpine plants can dominate—alpine azalea and diapensia. Both of these plants have tightly packed, waxy, evergreen leaves only about .25 inches in length; the form and size help the plants resist desiccation and withstand ice-blasting winter winds. Of all the alpine plants, the azalea has the tiniest flowers, which are only about .25 inches in diameter. In a good bloom year the alpine azalea can be covered with blossoms, making it look like the ground has simply been painted pink. The pink of the azaleas along with the diapensia's white blooms make the fellfields a sight to behold, especially considering the extreme environment in which these plants grow.

In areas that are not quite as windy and hold a small amount of snow cover, you will encounter meadows dominated by Bigelow's sedge—the most common sedge in the alpine zone of Mount Washington.

▲ The tiny pink blossoms of alpine azalea are the smallest of alpine flowers.

▲ Diapensia has a distinctive white blossom.

▲ Despite its name, alpine bluet has white flowers.

▲ Lapland rosebay's showy flowers accent a bed of lichen.

▲ Mountain heather sports distinctive bright pink blossoms.

▲ Bog bilberry and its round white blooms spread across a lichen-covered slab of granite.

In spots that hold more snow, you will find a variety of plants, including sedges, mosses, lichens, shrubs, and other pink and white wildflowers. One of these is the alpine bluet, which belies its name by often bearing pure white blossoms. You may also encounter the beautiful pink flowers of mountain heather, with foliage that looks like a spike of moss, as well as Lapland rosebay, with its large, showy blooms. A common shrub seen in this community is bog bilberry, which features round flowers that look more like white berries. It is a close relative of the blueberry. Most of the flowering plants mentioned above are pan-boreal across the northern hemisphere, and find their southern range limits in eastern North America, specifically the high peaks of New York, Vermont, New Hampshire, and Maine.

Walking through the Alpine Garden in late June, your gaze will be drawn downward to the bold, blooming, miniature plants. However, taking in the larger landscape view is also worthwhile. Looking up toward what is affectionately called the Rock Pile—the summit cone of Mount Washington—you will be able to see snowfields and pockets of stunted trees of black spruce and balsam fir. Known as *krummholz*,

▲ The Rock Pile, or summit cone, of Mount Washington. Notice the snow-fields and islands of krummholz.

▲ A very old balsam fir krummholz finds some protection next to a granite boulder.

▲ False hellebore and mountain avens grow in the foreground of this snow bed community.

a German term for twisted wood, these undersized trees exist in areas that capture deeper snow to protect themselves from ice-blasting winds that can strip their branches of needles.

Sometimes krummholz will occur as individual trees that gain a small amount of protection from boulders, generally on their western side, where the strongest winds blow. These trees will often be very contorted, hugging the ground. Although their stature is small they can be well over a century in age—a testament to their tenacity.

In deep snowfields that don't melt out until late spring or early summer, one can find snow bed communities that often hold lush vegetation common to lower elevations. Plants like false hellebore, rattlesnake root, and twisted stalk are common herbaceous species in this community, but no woody plants will be found because the growing season in a snow bed is so short. This is also where mountain avens—an herbaceous plant with bold buttercup-like flowers—is often seen. This species blooms later in summer and won't be in flower with the other small-statured, alpine plants. Although many of the alpine species can be found throughout the boreal region of the northern hemisphere, mountain avens is only found in the White Mountains of New Hampshire and three sites in Nova Scotia.

After about halfway down the Alpine Garden Trail, you will have passed by all the alpine communities and plants that occur here. If you wish, you can turn back and shorten your hike. However, I suggest continuing on to Tuckerman Ravine to see the impressive 1000-foot-deep bowl carved into the side of Mount Washington.

DRY RIVER
OLD GROWTH

Complex old-growth ecosystems on display

	DIFFICULTY
	Moderate

LOCATION ▸ Crawford Notch State Park, New Hampshire
FEATURES FOCUS ▸ Beech bark scale, old growth, tipped trees

LENGTH
2 miles

This hike is mostly level, but there is a section with irregular footing as the trail crosses old boulder bars from a previous channel of the Dry River.

During the late 1800s and early 1900s, a large portion of what is now the White Mountain National Forest was clear-cut. Luckily, the state of New Hampshire had already protected the forest on both sides of Crawford Notch, which included a large block of northern hardwood in an old-growth forest composed of American beech, sugar maple, yellow birch, and eastern hemlock. Old growth refers to a stand of trees that has reached maximal age without having any sign of disturbance during the tenure of the stand. Today, sections of both the Dry River and Saco River Trails go through this old-growth forest.

Start at the base of Crawford Notch on the Dry River Trail. As soon as you embark, evidence of old growth is visible: a long-in-the-tooth hemlock on the left side of the trail and just beyond it, an elderly yellow birch. Sadly, this forest has far fewer old-growth trees that it did in the mid-1900s. What used to be the most common old-growth tree in this forest—the American beech—no longer has any older specimens, due to the impacts of beech bark scale disease.

This disease has created what is commonly known as a beech hell—a dense understory of root-sprouted beech created by the disease. Because of the dense shade this understory beech hell creates and its dense network of surficial roots, no other plants can colonize this area. In turn, this allows beech trees to behave like an aggressive exotic species.

Continuing down the Dry River Trail, you will come upon sections where portions of the trail are eroded. This is from a damaging flood the day before Halloween in 2017. The dramatic impacts of that flood can be seen where the trail used to be, adjacent to the river shortly after the trail leaves Crawford Notch State Park and enters the National Forest. About a half mile down the Dry River Trail, you will come to a junction with the Saco River Trail. Continue down the Dry River Trail to see the flood impacts a bit farther along. On your way to the flood impacts, keep an eye on the right for a small stand of old-growth hemlock. These trees can be identified by their coarse bark plates, separated by horizontal fissures. Such fissures do not develop on hemlock bark until the trees are approaching 200 years of age.

A couple hundred yards past the hemlocks, you will enter a much younger forest with paper birch trees. These were generated by clear-cutting more than a century ago. At this point, you will have left the state park and will shortly come to the Dry River, with a large swath of boulders exposed by the 2017 flood. The Dry River Trail used to run through a section of forest where that boulder field now lies.

▴ A large hemlock shows the coarse bark plates separated by horizontal fissures that indicate the tree is near 200 years old.

▴ A stand of old-growth hemlocks near the Dry River Trail.

For long sections along the river, the original trail no longer exists, making a hike along the river a very challenging endeavor. The flood was sparked by a 3.5-inch downpour that followed a week of heavy precipitation. These boulder fields will in time develop soil, and the forest will return, as you will see when you backtrack down to the Saco River Trail.

When you return to the Saco River Trail, turn right. At first the going will be slow, because the trail runs across old boulder fields from a previous channel of the Dry River. Take your time on this section of trail; the footing is tricky. This trail is also not used a lot by hikers, so it can be hard to find. Be sure to keep an eye peeled for the blue trail blazes and areas on the ground that have exposed roots from previous hikers. Once you leave the boulder fields, the trail becomes quite easy to traverse. Keep an eye on the left for an old-growth yellow birch with a large burl on the side of its trunk. The bark of this tree looks far more like that of an old-growth sugar maple, but gazing up you may see catkins, confirming it is a birch.

▲ A boulder field on the Dry River was exposed by erosion from a 2017 flood.

Like black birch, the bark of yellow birch, as it ages, changes to look like another species of tree. To produce bark that looks like this takes a yellow birch over 200 years.

Continuing down the trail another 200 feet or so, you will come to an old-growth sugar maple on the right. You may also see a number of large, downed trees, the remains of dead beech. Soon after the sugar maple is an intersection with Maggie's Run. Continue on the Saco River Trail. Look for a large glacial boulder on the left, then a sugar maple tipped at roughly a 45-degree angle by a strong gust of wind. Unlike most tipped trees, this one retained its original trunk and the lowest limb did not have to become the trunk. Looking at this tree, contemplate the amount of weight that is cantilevered out away from its root system and how the tree has managed to stay standing. What you are witnessing is an example of biological cognizance.

Biological cognizance is the ability of species to receive information from their environment and then respond correctly to that information. Every organism is biologically cognizant. One cannot exist in an ecosystem and be oblivious of what is happening around it. Natural selection will quickly remove such individuals. An organism does not need a brain to be biologically cognizant. In fact, in our culture a brain may be an impediment to biological cognizance, because we are receiving a lot of very clear messages from our environment

▲ An old-growth yellow birch with a burl and bark that looks like a sugar maple.

▲ This sugar maple was tipped by strong wind and is supporting a huge amount of cantilevered weight.

that we are ignoring—a maladaptive and dangerous strategy. As for the sugar maple, when it was tipped, it sensed the new pull of gravity and readjusted its root system, tension, and compression wood to compensate. Today it is perfectly fine due to adjustments that were directed by its biological cognizance.

You will continue to see lots of downed trees and branches, known as coarse woody debris, or CWD. Old-growth stands have high amounts of CWD, which boosts the species richness of the surrounding area as the coarse woody debris creates microenvironments for decomposing species. During November of 2019, I conducted a course for the Oak Spring Foundation in Virginia that was attended by two arborists from England. I was amazed to hear them talking about pruning large dead trees in England to keep them standing, as a means of supporting a richer community of decomposers. They mentioned that some of the old snags hosted over 20,000 species! That arborists would work to intentionally maintain such high biodiversity in dead snags was notable; it showed that their training was very much ecologically inspired. Today many landowners like whole-tree harvesting, since it leaves their forests looking neat and tidy. However, a healthy forest is a messy one. By removing CWD, forests become simplified and far less resilient, not unlike a compromised immune system.

In time, the trail will cross an ephemeral stream and you will come to more old-growth hemlock on the left and old-growth white pine on the right. You can continue on the Saco River Trail to the Webster Cliff Trail and pass through some more pockets of old growth, or return the way you came. When you do come to the Dry River Trail, be sure to take a hard right back to the trailhead on Route 302 and not the trail that leads back to the Dry River Campground.

▲ A downed old-growth trunk is coarse woody debris, which provides a microenvironment for thousands of species of fungi, bacteria, and invertebrates.

PHILBRICK-CRICENTI BOG

Curiosities of bog life and nature's affinity for math

DIFFICULTY
Easy

LENGTH
1 mile

LOCATION ▸ New London, New Hampshire

FEATURES FOCUS ▸ Math in nature

This short walk on a boardwalk and forest trails leads to a beautiful bog. The best time to visit is in mid- to late June, when the bloom is at its height.

Philbrick-Cricenti Bog is probably the least-known site covered in this book and as such, may be a bit harder to locate than the others. It is cared for, and its boardwalk is maintained, by the New London Conservation Commission. This group deserves a lot of credit for making this gem of a bog open to the public.

▴ Keep an eye out for blooming calla lily.

The trailhead lies along the south side of Newport Road, about a quarter mile from the junction with New London's Main Street. There is a kiosk at the start of the trail, but it may be difficult to see from the road. The trail starts in a red maple swamp on a boardwalk just two planks wide, so a single file procession is necessary here. Please be sure to stay on the boardwalk; stepping off will seriously impact this bog's fragile vegetation. As you proceed, the pH of the site decreases and larch, black spruce, and sheep laurel start to replace the red maple. If you are there in June keep an eye out for calla lily, with its elegant white blooms. The calla is actually not a lily, but rather a member of the arum family; each flower has a spikelike spadix wrapped in its spathe. Soon you will come to a junction; at this point go to the left on the Tundra Garden Loop.

You will transition out of the forest and into the bog, coming to groves of small black spruce and larch, stands of larger trees of these species, and patches of bog, all in a wonderful mixture of wetland ecosystems. The placement of these different wetlands is based on how much peat has accumulated underneath them—the more peat, the more stable the substrate, and the larger the vegetation. Bogs create peat, which is partially decomposed plant material. Species of sphagnum moss make up a major portion of peat, which can absorb large amounts of water.

▲ The boardwalk emerges into a mix of bog and different sized tree communities.

In this transitional area you will also start to see classic bog vegetation like round-leaved sundews. Similar to pitcher plants, sundews are carnivorous and get their nutrients via insects, not roots. This is because nutrients in acidic bogs are so limited, plant roots are unable to derive sustenance. In the case of our native sundews, circular-shaped leaves are surrounded by tentacles tipped with a drop of sundew—a very sticky liquid. Once an insect gets stuck on a tentacle, the other tentacles then push the insect toward the center of the leaf, which slowly wraps around the bug and even more slowly digests it for nutrients.

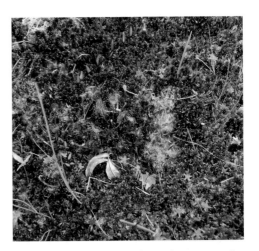

▲ Sticky, insect-trapping tentacles can be seen extending from round-leaved sundews that are thriving in a mat of sphagnum moss.

Studies of one of Tasmania's sundew species have shown that when one of its tentacles comes in contact with an insect, it can snap that tentacle inward toward the heart of the leaf in 75 microseconds. Our sundews are far more relaxed.

June is a great time to visit this bog—just about all of its flowering plants are in bloom then, including sheep laurel, pitcher plants, and small cranberry. Another plant blooming then is the orchid grass

▲ Sheep laurel makes a pretty pink show in June.

▲ Grass pink is an easily identified orchid in New England bogs.

pink, also known as calopogon, which means "beautiful beard." The beard reference is a nod to this orchid's anvil-shaped lip, from which grows a dense cluster of yellow-tipped stamens. Grass pink is the most common orchid growing in our regional bogs and is found throughout Philbrick-Cricenti.

In time, you will come to the Quaking Loop that will take you the farthest out into the open bog. Two other bog plants can be seen here—bog laurel and bog rosemary—which, if you are visiting in June, will likely not be in bloom. Both plants have very similar long, narrow, light green leaves. The easiest way to distinguish them is that bog laurel's leaves are oppositely arranged, meaning they come off opposing sides of a twig at the same spot, while bog rosemary's leaves are alternately arranged. Although bog rosemary has a nice scent, it is quite toxic and should not be collected as an herb for cooking. From the Quaking Loop, you can look over the open bog to the tree swamp that rims it. The tree swamp is composed of black spruce and larch.

Eventually the trail will leave the bog and enter a forest composed of red maple and balsam fir. In the chapter on Orono Bog in Maine, I discuss the resin blisters unique to balsam fir, which are used for protection from bark beetles. These bark blisters are also visible on balsam fir here. On some of the younger trees in this forest, it's possible to see horizontal lenticels, which are used for bark photosynthesis. Look closely and you will see that each lenticel is the juncture of a clockwise and counterclockwise spiral.

If you count the number of clockwise spirals of lenticels going around a tree and then count the number of counterclockwise spirals, you will always get two consecutive numbers in the Fibonacci sequence of mathematical fame. The sequence is made up of numbers that are the sum of the two preceding numbers. For example, 0, 1, 1, 2, 3, 5, 8, and 13 are part of the Fibonacci sequence. After the number 5 in the series, each subsequent pair of numbers will create a ratio that fluctuates close to .617. This is known as the golden mean. For example, the ratio of 5 to 8 is .625, and 8 to 13 is .615.

▲ The open bog is edged by a tree swamp composed of black spruce and larch.

This mathematical sequence is present throughout nature. For example, all interlocking right-hand and left-hand spirals found in nature are based on two consecutive numbers in the Fibonacci sequence. This is true for the spiraling scales in pitch pine cones and the seed pattern in the head of a sunflower, just to name a couple. Single spirals in nature also are based on this series.

The trail through the forest will bring you back to the Tundra Garden Loop. From there, you can do the Peek Hole Loop, where you can probe the depth of the bog with a long stick that has been inserted in the bog for that purpose, and then continue on to the Bog Peril Loop. Although not as open or diverse as the Quaking Loop, these loops are fun to explore. On the way to the Bog Peril Loop, you will come to many highbush blueberries that have witches' brooms—tight, dense clusters of twigs. Such growths are the result of a rust fungus that also spends part of its life in balsam fir trees. The rust essentially creates a tumorous growth on the blueberry, but on the balsam fir, it can result in needle cast—the yellowing and dropping of needles. Although witches' broom can parasitize highbush blueberries, they rarely kill them.

Even during times when plants are not in bloom, this bog is worthy of exploration, with its reddish sphagnum mosses, dwarfed trees, sundews, and evergreen members of the heath family.

MANCHESTER CEDAR SWAMP

DIFFICULTY
Moderate

Urban swamp with tree-bark reading lessons

LENGTH
2 miles

LOCATION ▸ Manchester, New Hampshire
FEATURES FOCUS ▸ Chestnut blight, glacial impact, grafting, Great NE
Hurricane of 1938, old growth, stump sprouts, tipped trees, tree
secrets: black gum

U nlike most sites covered in this book, parking for this exploration is limited at the trailhead. The route is over fairly level
terrain with some sections of irregular footing.

Located just a couple of miles from the heart of New Hampshire's
largest city, the Manchester Cedar Swamp Preserve is a unique mix
of forest and wetland ecosystems covering roughly one square mile.
Protected by The Nature Conservancy, this parcel offers a wonderful
wilderness retreat adjacent to a large metropolitan city.

The trail begins in a hemlock stand and leads to the Woodland
Loop—the first of three loop trails you will explore. Just before
you get to the junction with this loop trail, keep an eye out for a
white pine tipped toward the northwest by winds out of the southeast. Stand-leveling winds from that direction are the result of the
infrequent hurricanes—occurring about once every 125 years—that
make it this far into New England. This pine was tipped as a young
tree at around 6 p.m., September 21, 1938 in an especially deadly
hurricane.

The Great New England Hurricane of 1938 traveled across New
England at unusually high speeds. It made landfall near New Haven,
Connecticut in the afternoon of September 21, and was moving into
Canada only six hours later. Its velocity allowed the storm to remain
a hurricane 200 miles from where it made landfall, creating forest
blowdowns and serious infrastructure damage in its wake. Sadly,
nearly 700 people died in the storm.

At the junction with the Woodland Loop, go right and follow the yellow blazes. As you start this loop, you will be in a dry woodland dominated by oaks, both red and white. Like many of New England's natural sites, this woodland is strewn with granite, glacial boulders that create some sections of irregular footing.

Keep an eye out for numerous American chestnut sprouts—the remnants of an impressive tree that was severely impacted by the introduction of the exotic chestnut blight fungus from Asia into New York in 1904. Asian chestnuts had coevolved with this fungus to the point that it was merely a mild parasite. However, American chestnut trees greater than 10 inches in diameter were quickly killed. Smaller trees had their trunks girdled (cambium beneath bark destroyed in a ring around the trunk) by the fungus, but their roots were not killed and could send up stump sprouts from the base of the tree. The tiny sprouts you will see are growing from root systems that are well over 100 years of age and have stump sprouted maybe a dozen or more times as their young trunks have been repeatedly killed by the fungus. These chestnuts will keep repeating this cycle until they get overtopped by a hemlock, a tree that can create enough shade to restrict stump sprouting. To see a photo of a chestnut stump sprout, go to the chapter on Monument Mountain in Massachusetts.

The introduction of the chestnut blight was possibly the most damaging event to impact the temperate deciduous forest of eastern North America in thousands, possibly millions, of years. At the time of the introduction, the chestnut was one of the most common tree species in the heart of the temperate forest of the eastern United States. It was also one of the largest broad-leaved trees in the region, growing to over 12 feet in diameter. It was a very important tree to humans and wildlife alike, thanks to edible nuts that were prolifically produced by the species. This signature tree of the temperate decidu-ous forest was almost completely removed in just 30 years, following the blight's introduction. Luckily, some American chestnuts were able to resist the blight. Since 2012 I have encountered five stands of chestnut trees that have resisted the blight for many decades and reached reproductive age. Chestnuts need to cross-pollinate to make viable nuts, so in these stands there are seedlings and saplings that may have a higher degree of resistance than their parent trees. I am hopeful that after many generations in these stands, truly resistant

^ Reddish orange cyanobacteria can be seen in the bark fissures of a red oak.

American chestnuts will emerge and start to expand their populations. My guess is that there are a lot more resistant stands out there than the few I have found.

As you hike along, you will be able to identify red oaks by the reddish orange cyanobacteria that grow in their bark fissures. Not all red oaks have this cyanobacteria, but because the bacteria is host specific, when you see it on a tree's bark, it means the tree is a red oak. Like lichens, the cyanobacteria most likely helps its host tree by increasing nutrient availability, creating a mutually beneficial relationship.

In time you will come to the junction with the Cedar Loop Trail and will turn right. When you reach the actual loop part of the trail, go right again to do the loop in a counterclockwise fashion. Watch for white pine seedlings and saplings in the understory. When I was a student at the University of New Hampshire in the early 1970s, we were instructed that we would never find white pine seedlings growing in the understory of an oak forest. Sure enough, every oak forest we visited at that time had no understory white pine. The oak leaf litter kept the white pine seeds from accessing exposed soil that would help them establish. However, today it is common to see white pine in the understory of an oak forest. What has changed? It was the reintroduction of a native species: the wild turkey. Turkeys, as they forage, scratch up the leaf litter to find insects and seeds, creating patches of exposed soil. When the turkeys were absent, no one knew what an important species they are for creating germination sites for all sorts of plants that have small seeds. In point of fact, they play a major role in boosting the plant species diversity in the understory of our woodlands.

When you come to a small bridge crossing a stream, on the left you will find an old black gum with deeply fissured bark. Black gums with bark this coarse are well over 300 years old, possibly closer to 400 years. To estimate the age of a tree, consider not just how big the tree is but also the coarseness of its bark. Within a species, all trees produce the same thickness of bark each year, but the amount of wood they produce can be highly variable. Trees growing in good sites, with ample light, moisture, and nutrients, can produce a lot of wood each growing season, laying down big annual growth rings. On trees like this, the bark is stretched, making it appear less coarse than you might think it should be for a tree of its size. However, for trees on poor sites that lay down little wood, the bark is not stretched and builds up coarse plates with deep fissures. Old-growth trees that also grow slowly

▲ This black gum has the coarse bark plates and fissures that suggest it is quite old.

produce very coarse bark like this black gum. In New Hampshire, black gums can reach the greatest age of any tree species—around 700 years.

Soon you will come to the boardwalk that goes through the Manchester Cedar Swamp. The canopy of this swamp is shared by Atlantic white cedars and red maple. The understory hosts cinnamon ferns, skunk cabbage, and rhododendron. This last species can be identified by its long, evergreen leaves, which are larger than those found on any of our other regional shrubs. Rhododendron is extensively discussed in the chapter on Rhododendron State Park, which is also in New Hampshire.

Although the cedars in this swamp are not huge, they are old, based on their significant bark spirals. On most trees, trunk spirals are only seen when they are either scarred by lightning or exist as snags that have dropped their bark. On cedars, the bark also follows the spiral of the trunk's wood. Most tree trunks spiral to the right as one looks up. From my experience, Atlantic white cedar is the only regional species that more frequently spirals to the left. Although the direction of the spiral is genetically determined, the intensity of the twist is a result of environmental factors.

▲ Left-hand spirals, as in the bark of this old Atlantic white cedar, are fairly rare.

▲ Based on its coarse bark plates, this small red oak is likely much older than its overall size suggests.

Trunks grow in a spiral to keep limbs from growing directly above one another. If, during growth, a tree elongates its trunk quickly, the tightness of the twist is reduced. If the elongation is slower, the spiral is tighter, making the trunk stronger. Trees that have strong trunk spirals are often those that are suppressed by the canopy or heavy winds, are open-grown trees expanding outward rather than upward, or are old trees that have stopped increasing their height.

When you return to the Woodland Loop, take a right and look for some old red oaks with coarse bark plates that are slightly less than a foot in diameter. This is an example of how one needs to look at bark, not just size, to estimate the age of trees. These small oaks are probably close to 150 years old, while a normal red oak of this size would be more like 30 years young.

Head right when you reach the Rhododendron Loop. You will enter a hemlock forest and follow the blue blazes. This will eventually take you into a power line cut (an area cleared for an electrical line route) with dry, acidic soils. This can be discerned by two species that grow here—sweet fern and bear oak. Sweet fern is not a fern but a flowering shrub related to bayberry. If you rub the outer twigs of this species, you will get an aromatic scent that is the origin of the word "sweet" in this species' common name. Bear oak has leaves similar to red oak in shape, but it can be identified by leaves that are shiny on top and light colored underneath. Red oak leaves are the same color on both sides. Since bear oaks rarely grow more than 15 feet in height, bears can eat acorns right off their low branches, thus the tree's name.

Leaving the power line cut, you will cross a wetland then head back into the power line cut. Once through the cut this second time, you will come to the loop portion of this trail, with a dense stand of rhododendrons on the right. A good time to do this trail is in early July, when these plants will support a showy bloom of pink and white flowers. Go left on the loop trail to do it in a clockwise fashion. About 100 feet from the loop junction, you will come to the start of a small esker: a snaking, small ridge composed of sand and gravel that was created by a subglacial stream.

Glacial ice holds all sorts of materials, from clay to boulders. As a glacier withers, crevices cut down through it, carrying meltwater. When the meltwater reaches the bottom, it forms a subglacial stream. The stream's velocity then slows, depositing the sand and gravel it carries in the streambed. As more material is deposited, the stream-bed grows upward, pushing the stream higher into the glacier. Over time, when the glacier melts away, it leaves an esker—a meandering ridge that was the old subglacial streambed. After the trail leaves the esker, the rest of the Rhododendron Loop is quite homogeneous, so if you want to shorten your hike, turn around and head back into the power line cut.

Once you have passed through the power line cut twice on your return, you will reenter the hemlock forest. When you do, note a seep (a small spring or wet area) to the left of the trail. About 50 feet past this seep, look for a hemlock stump adjacent to the swamp, on the right. This was a tree that was cut years ago, but is not dead, as is evident by the growth of its callus wood over the cut. So how can a stump, without any way to photosynthesize, stay alive and slowly grow? The answer is that this tree was root grafted onto a neighbor-ing tree or trees before it was cut. Once the tree was cut, the neigh-boring trees supplied the stump with energy and kept it alive. The bark covering the callus wood of hemlocks lays down annual growth

▴ A hemlock wound shows three distinct bark lines on its callus wood.

▴ A series of curved cracks in the bark of a red maple reveals that it once had target canker fungus.

lines that are often easily seen many decades following the wound that created them. On this stump, the callus wood's bark shows no annual growth lines and most of the wood of the original stump has rotted away. A stump with these features was cut more than 40 years ago. A photo of a root-grafted hemlock can be seen in the chapter on Pisgah State Park, also in New Hampshire.

Many of our trees growing within 10–15 feet of each other root graft. This can happen between species and even between broad-leaved trees and conifers. One of my former graduate students used to own Bug Hill Farm in Ashfield, Massachusetts. On a trail on the far side of a beaver pond on that property, we came upon two neighboring trees that were uprooted—a hemlock and a yellow birch. These two trees had a clear graft, where a root of each tree seamlessly joined into a single root that connected the two trees.

If you look to the left of the root-grafted hemlock stump, you will see a wound on the trunk of a neighboring hemlock that shows clear bark lines on the callus wood. When I saw this tree in 2019, I could clearly count three bark lines, meaning the tree was wounded in 2016.

When you return to the Woodland Loop, go right to continue back to the parking lot. Along the way, watch for a red maple on the right side of the trail that has an intricate pattern on its bark. The pattern is a series of cracks in the bark that follow each other in a curving fashion. This is the result of red maple target canker that is host specific to this tree. The name of the fungus is derived from the fact that it sometimes creates a series of circular cracks, one inside another, making it look like a target with a bull's eye. The fungus is active on the surface of the smooth bark of young red maples, and when alive, it looks like circular white lines. After the fungus dies and the bark starts maturing, its fissures follow where the fungal lines used to be. Not all red maples host target canker, but when you see this pattern on the bark of a tree, you can be sure it is a red maple.

RHODODENDRON STATE PARK

DIFFICULTY
Easy

LENGTH
.75 miles

Regal rhododendrons; traces of long-ago farms

LOCATION ▸ Fitzwilliam, New Hampshire
FEATURES FOCUS ▸ Great NE Hurricane of 1938, pillows and cradles, stone walls and early agriculture, tree secrets: black gum

This is a level loop on smooth trails.

In the New England states of Vermont, New Hampshire, and Maine, there are six sites that have rhododendrons. At 16 acres, Rhododendron State Park hosts the largest population of this species in all of northern New England. The best time to visit this park is in early to mid-July, when these large shrubs put forth a dramatic floral display.

This exploration starts on the Little Monadnock Mountain Trail, whose trailhead is centrally located in the parking area. When you reach the first rhododendron, look to the right for a big pine snag where half the trunk—on the side facing the trail—is missing. This was the result of a lightning strike. When lightning hits a live tree, it doesn't spark a fire, but in microseconds it turns the sap into steam. If the charge just runs along one side of a tree, the steam will blow off the bark, and sometimes the wood, along its path on the trunk. However, if the charge runs along the whole tree, the steam explosion will blow the tree apart, as it did with this white pine. Besides often being the tallest trees in the forest canopy, white pines are also good conductors because of their abundant sap. For these reasons, they are especially likely to be hit by lightning. So remember: if you get caught in a forest during a thunderstorm, stay away from tall white pines.

When you reach the first trail junction, turn right on the Little Monadnock Mountain Trail. Eventually you will come to the junction with the Rhododendron Loop Trail, where you will turn left and

quickly be swallowed up by rhododendron. The tall shrub creates a
tunnel for the trail to pass through, making a walk in this forest a
very unique experience. As you move along under the rhododendron,
notice how dense these shrubs are and that nothing grows underneath them. The density of these stands is related to the fact that
rhododendrons can layer and are very shade tolerant. Layering is an
adaptation in which branches that touch the ground can send down
roots at that point, allowing the plant to create clones.

Another unique feature of the rhododendron is its leaves.
Leathery and evergreen, rhododendron leaves are the largest of any
evergreen species in the temperate deciduous forest of eastern North
America. This is a great adaptation for an understory species because
it allows the plants to dramatically increase photosynthesis, particularly in early spring and late fall, when the canopy leaves are not
present. Another member of the heath family that has the second-
largest evergreen leaves is also encountered on this trail—mountain
laurel. Thanks to the increased amount of photosynthesis that both

▲ The trail passes
through a tun-
nel formed by
rhododendrons.

▲ Rhododendrons in bloom are hard to miss.

▲ Rhododendron floral heads here are large and usually whitish pink.

of these shrubs accomplish, they can do something that other under-story shrubs in our region can't: produce dramatic flowers. Going into a hardwood forest with an understory of mountain laurel in late May, or one with rhododendron in mid-July, can be reminiscent of a late-season snow. However, there is a liability to large evergreen leaves. Species like these are restricted to warmer sites, where cold winter nights will not desiccate their leaves. In response to this potential problem, when it gets cold, rhododendron leaves curl into slender, tubular shapes that reduce surface area to resist desiccation and help shed snow.

Soon the trail will emerge from the forest and cross a bridge that is adjacent to a black gum swamp. If you look at the canopies of the black gum, you will see they are quite deformed. Since they are a long-lived species and have brittle wood, they experience a lot of trunk breakage after many years. Past the swamp, you will come to a trail junction. At this point go straight onto the Wildflower Trail.

A short way down the Wildflower Trail, you will cross a stone wall. Nearby, this wall forms a corner with another. Once you cross the wall, the ground becomes smooth and even on the surface, indi-cating that its pillows and cradles (mounds and pits in the terrain where live trees have toppled along with their root masses) have been removed by previous plowing of the ground. A look at the stone wall to the right reveals that there are a lot of small, fist-sized stones in the middle of the wall. This indicates that the site was originally a crop field and the stones were removed from the field for farming.

Farther along the stone wall, where the trail starts to turn to the left, you will see a white pine with a number of large, dead lower limbs that are being grown over. These indicate that this tree grew in the open and put its energy into growing outward with large, low branches rather than racing straight up to the canopy. Because there are low limbs all the way around the tree, we can deduce that when it was young, there was no forest on either side of the wall. The side of the wall with the trail is the former crop field. Because a wall was built along the crop field, it suggests that the other side of it was pasture, with the wall being built to keep livestock out of the crops. If the far side was either always forested or a hayfield, there would have been no need to put in the labor of building a wall. It would have been easier to simply dump the stone along the edge of the crop field.

▴ The gnarled canopy of a black gum can be seen through a rhododendron's distinctive leaves.

As the trail turns away from the wall, look to the left for a yellow birch with aboveground roots that are growing down into a mound with a downed trunk emerging from it. This tree was blown down by southeast winds generated by the Great New England Hurricane of 1938 that was discussed in the previ-

▴ Between the visible large stones that anchor this rock wall are scores of smaller, fist-sized stones removed from the crop field that once abutted the wall.

ous chapter. When the tree fell down, its roots stood up out of the ground, holding dirt in its root mass. This exposed dirt was a good germination site for the shade-tolerant, small-seeded yellow birch that established here, snaking its roots down toward the ground. When the downed tree's root system rotted away, it left this stilted-rooted

▸ clockwise from left An open-grown white pine with large, low limbs suggests that when it was young, there was no forest around it. ▪ A tipped red maple blown over by New England's 1938 hurricane. Its lowest branch grew up and turned into the tree's new trunk. ▪ This stone pile is composed of small rocks collected from a former crop field. Because they were not removed, the field was most likely converted to a pasture around the time of the Civil War.

birch. A bit farther along, on the right, you will see a red maple that was also blown over by the hurricane. Unlike the previous downed tree, this one didn't die and its lowest living limb took off growing upward—becoming the fallen tree's new trunk.

After you pass the blown-over red maple, keep an eye on the left side of the trail for a pile of small stones. This is another indication of the former crop field. Small stone piles are often found on ledges within a crop field; remnants of ridding the field of rocks. However, this pile is on the ground. Each year after plowing, exposed rocks were gathered in piles so they could be loaded on a stone "boat" or sled and dragged away. Since this pile was not removed, it indicates that the crop field was abandoned that same year and most likely converted to pasture, probably sometime around the Civil War.

Up until the mid-1800s, most of our regional farms had many acres dedicated to growing grains. Flax was grown not only for grain, but also for the fiber in its stem that went into making linen. In the early 1800s, it took about 2 acres of flax to produce enough fiber to make a single bed sheet. So, many farms had a lot of acres solely in flax. Growing grain was the most laborious activity on a farm. Large acreages were plowed, the exposed rocks removed, seeds sown, the crop tended. At harvest time, all those acres were scythed, and finally the grain was winnowed. In the 1860s, when rail had linked up rural communities with urban centers, New England farms converted to dairy farming, as rail transported milk products quickly into cities. Rail also allowed grains being grown out West to be brought to New England. Farmers decided to take proceeds from their dairy sales and simply buy the western grain, converting crop fields into pastures or hayfields that took a lot less work to manage.

Shortly after passing the small stone pile, the ground will change from smooth to lumpy, from residual pillows and cradles. This means that you have either crossed into an abandoned pasture or a wood-lot that was never cleared for agriculture, because the ground was never plowed. If this area was a former pasture, you would expect a wall to separate it from the crop field. But no evidence of a stone wall is visible. That would make the woodlot a good guess, except for another clue. The forest that now grows on this spot is dominated by weevil-hit white pines that are about 80 years old, indicating that this was once open land that wasn't abandoned to forest until around 1940. The lack of a stone fence between the abandoned pasture and crop field means one of two things: the fence that separated these two sites was made of wood, not stone, and has decayed away, or when the crop field was converted to pasture, it was expanded into this area of pillows and cradles.

When the Wildflower Trail reaches the next intersection, you can go right to head back to the parking lot or take a left to explore some short interior trails loaded with more groves of the magnificent rhododendron.

PISGAH STATE PARK

DIFFICULTY
Difficult

Climb Mount Pisgah through old-growth stands

LENGTH
4 miles

LOCATION ‣ Hinsdale, New Hampshire
FEATURES FOCUS ‣ Grafting, Great NE Hurricane of 1938, old growth, pillows and cradles, tree secrets: black birch

This is a challenging round-trip trail over irregular terrain. The climb to the summit of Mount Pisgah is a moderate ascent up a few hundred feet.

Start at Kilburn Road trailhead, off Route 63, a few miles south of Chesterfield, New Hampshire. For this entire hike, you will be in an area of over 5000 acres that was never cleared for agricultural activity, making it the largest low-elevation site of its kind in the region. Because of this, there are a number of old-growth stands, although not as many as there were prior to the Great New England Hurricane of 1938—a possible category 4 storm that wreaked havoc throughout the area and killed nearly 700 people. This exploration will go through one of the old-growth pockets of trees.

You'll begin on a very well-built woods road. There is an unusual reason for the high quality of this road that will be discovered about a mile from the trailhead. Most of this exploration will be through hemlock-dominated forests—a result of the woodlands' age. Hemlock is the region's most competitive tree, and given enough time without major disturbances, will often monopolize forests. Along with hemlock, you will see mountain laurel as well. Walking down the road, look to your left for two tipped hemlocks. The longer downed trunk is pointing to a live, root-grafted hemlock stump on the other side of the road.

Even though the stump is the result of its original trunk being cut down, the tree was root grafted onto the tree immediately next to it before it was cut. That adjacent tree supplied the stump with energy and kept it alive.

At the height of the land, the road turns to the right and then a bit farther on turns to the left. Close to this left turn in the road, look to the right to see a hemlock that has many healed-over wounds from cavities excavated by pileated woodpeckers. The pileated woodpecker is the largest member of the woodpecker family in the Northeast. It creates large, rectangular holes in search of its chief prey—carpenter ants. These birds can excavate a lot of wood from a tree and the impact may appear damaging. However, they can actually help a tree if they extinguish the carpenter ant colony. When this happens in a hemlock, all of the pecked holes will heal over. In this tree's case, there are some new excavations by woodpeckers, and in time their efforts may curtail the ant colony.

The road now begins its final descent to Kilburn Pond. At the junction with Kilburn Loop Trail, go left and pass a small fen (marshy low land) succeeding to a tree swamp on your left. Soon, on the right, the road will come upon Baker Brook flowing into Kilburn Pond. At this point, look for a number of small hemlocks between the road and the stream. You'll see that these trees have had their bark removed around the base of their trunks; it is girdling by a beaver and is often seen in hemlocks that grow around a beaver's pond.

⁕ The longer downed trunk points to a root-grafted hemlock stump.

⁕ A portion of this hemlock stump root-grafted to the tree behind it and is still slowly growing.

⁕ Healed-over holes of a pileated woodpecker looking for carpenter ants in a hemlock. If the ants are eradicated, the woodpecker will have done the tree a favor.

It's important to note that the beaver didn't invest the energy to cut these trees down—doing just enough damage to kill them—because beavers are not fond of hemlock bark as a winter food supply. The question is, Why did the beaver not just leave these trees alone? The answer is that the beaver is trying to get rid of the hemlock in order to benefit more of the animal's favored trees for winter food: hardwoods. Hemlocks produce dense shade, and as mentioned, are not the beaver's favorite winter sustenance. Hardwoods, on the other hand, offer a longer-lasting winter food supply. Hardwoods also stump sprout (producing more potential beaver food) when cut—*if* they have enough light. By removing the shade-producing hemlock and encouraging their preferred hardwoods to stump sprout, the beaver is managing for a better, more enduring winter pantry.

Soon you will come to a trail junction with the Town Forest Trail, which goes straight, while the Kilburn Loop Trail crosses the stream. Take the Town Forest Trail to discover why the road you walked in on was so well constructed. In time, on the right side of the trail, you will come to two unusual concrete structures. Both have double wall construction with heavily reinforced rebar to make them very strong. You should be able to see that the inner walls of both structures were damaged by an explosion. The blast bowed the walls outward and exposed their rebar.

What you have encountered are prototypes for bunkers to house military supplies. In the 1960s, these were built and tested to withstand an internal explosion. This spot was chosen since it was a mile from any residences and had ample sand, gravel, and water on-site to make concrete. The road was constructed to bring in the cement, rebar, and other materials. Not exactly part of an ecosystem, but an unusual point of interest and worth the side trip.

Head back to the Kilburn Loop Trail, cross the bridge, and you will enter a stand composed solely of hemlock, both in the canopy and the understory. A close look at these understory hemlocks shows that many have flat tops, not the normal conical shape of a conifer. These are trees that have entered idling mode—a condition in which they are growing very slowly due to limited light. Understory trees like these can idle for decades, growing only a few feet tall and having trunks that are only an inch or so in diameter. The oldest idling hemlock I have aged was 120 years old—and only 6 feet in height.

Once you cross Baker Brook and leave Kilburn Road behind, you will enter a forest that very much feels like wilderness; this part of Pisgah State Park is truly a special environment. When you reach John Summers Trail on the right, keep left on Kilburn Loop Trail. At the next trail junction, leave Kilburn Loop Trail and go left onto the Pisgah Ridge Connector Trail, which will take you to Pisgah Ridge Trail. You will cross a second bridge and then about 100 feet before the third bridge, look to your left for an old-growth hemlock that has a basal scar on its trunk. This tree is over 300 years old and an indicator that you are approaching a stand of old-growth hemlock and white pine. Make a point of comparing the bark texture of this tree to the other hemlocks around it so you can develop an eye for how to identify old-growth hemlocks by their bark.

Soon you will come to the fourth bridge. The trail will then run along the base of the Pisgah ridgeline—a granite ridge that rises steeply to your right with scattered old-growth trees. The trail comes to a shrubby swamp on the left and you will cross a section

▲ A view of the Kilburn Loop Trail just before the junction with the Pisgah Ridge Connector Trail.

▲ An old-growth white pine on the way to the summit of Mount Pisgah.

of boardwalk. On the right, look for a large patch of trailing arbutus and if you happen to be there in April, bend down to catch the sweet scent of its flowers. Next you will climb into a small stand of old growth. Sadly, a number of the old hemlocks and pines were impacted by a microburst around 2015 that left just a handful of old-growth trees. The largest hemlock upslope on the right is approaching 350 years old. A close look at this tree will show chartreuse-colored, crustose lichen growing on its bark. In my experience, a hemlock has to reach an age of about 275 years before this lichen can grow on its bark. My guess is it takes that long to leach the tannin from the outer bark of the hemlock, allowing the lichen to colonize. About 100 feet farther up the trail are some old-growth white pines on both sides.

After these ancient pines, you will come to the junction with the Pisgah Ridge Trail. At this point you will enter a site that was not protected by the Pisgah ridgeline and was blown down by the 1938 hurricane—just hundreds of feet from old-growth trees that *were* protected by the ridge. Turn left on the Pisgah Ridge Trail and descend to a vernal pool in a forest of very deformed hemlocks. When my daughter was around 12 years old, we entered this stand and she said to me, "Dad, I think there must be an evil arborist around here." I don't know about evil, but the so-called arborists that impacted these trees are porcupines. These hemlocks have been browsed by porcupines for possibly a century or more.

Hemlocks are the porcupine's favorite tree, and they will visit repeatedly to eat the twigs. If the spiny creatures have denning sites in tree hollows, or in the boulder caves of a talus slope near a stand of hemlock, the trees become misshapen from generations of browsers. Studies have shown that porcupines have a higher frequency of bone fractures than any other regional wildlife species. The reason is that they venture far out on hemlock limbs, where taking a fall is more likely. At the base of the granite ledge to the right of the trail you can see boulder caves that have housed porcupines for centuries.

Just as the trail emerges from the contorted hemlocks, look to the right to see two very old black birch trees whose bark looks more like that of old oaks. To confirm that the trees are birches, look into their canopies to see their catkins or unlobed leaves. It takes a black birch up to 200 years to develop bark that has vertical ridges like an oak. These two birch trees are over 300 years of age—about as old as they get for this species.

▲ A stand of hemlock deformed by repeated browsing by porcupines.

After you pass the old black birch, the trail climbs to another portion of the ridgeline. You will come to a granite outcrop with a view toward Mount Monadnock in the east. This is one of the most pristine views one can get in New England. One distant farm and one tower are the only evidence of human presence from this vantage point. When you reach this outcrop, please keep your feet on the exposed bedrock at all times and definitely don't step into the fragile crevice communities that hold moss, reindeer lichen, and lowbush blueberry. Here the trail turns back into the woods. In a short distance, look for a cellar hole on the right side of the trail.

▲ An old-growth black birch with vertical bark ridges that look more like those of an oak.

A 130-year-old white pine was growing out of the foundation of this cellar hole in 2019, indicating the house that once stood here was gone by the late 1800s. A small section of the forest floor before the cellar hole and on the right side of the trail is smooth and even, with the exception of pillows formed by the 1938 hurricane. Looking around, you can also find scattered small stone piles, indicating someone was growing crops here. However, here there are no stone walls or evidence of any outbuildings, so the residents most likely had no livestock. This suggests that they tended their small crop field with a hoe.

Who would have farmed this remote ridgetop, surrounded by forest, miles from any neighbors, in the middle 1800s? I have a guess, but I'll let you ponder your own ideas. I will say the granite outcrop facing Mount Monadnock is an important feature of my hypothesis.

Now you can choose to continue on the Pisgah Ridge Trail to another viewpoint, more old-growth trees, and more porcupine-contorted hemlocks. Or if you want to summit Mount Pisgah for a more expansive view both to the east and west, you can turn around. If you choose to continue on the Pisgah Ridge Trail and not go for the summit, about a quarter mile farther down the trail you can turn left onto the Town Forest Trail and make a loop back to the bunkers. The rest of this chapter is devoted to what you will see if you summit Mount Pisgah.

Turning around from the homesite and reentering the stand of deformed hemlock, look for a nurse stump on the left with a hemlock growing on it. As the nurse stump decays, it will leave this stilted-root hemlock growing out of the ground. However, the main root on the left—growing out horizontally over the top of the stump and then down—indicates that the tree grew on the stump. Another way we can get stilted-root trees is from a nurse log, on top of which a number of trees have grown. In that case, when the nurse log rots away, a number of trees will be left growing in a line, with their aboveground roots stitching them together along the line. In New England, white pine and spruce most commonly serve as nurse stumps and nurse logs. Both decay slowly from the outside, giving ample time for small-seeded, shade-tolerant trees like yellow birch, black birch, and hemlock to establish.

▲ This hemlock tree is growing on a white pine nurse stump.

When you come back to the junction of the Pisgah Ridge Trail and the Pisgah Ridge Connector Trail at the old-growth stand, you can go straight on the Pisgah Ridge Trail to the summit of Mount Pisgah. This ten-minute climb is worth it for the view, which is more expansive than the perspective near the cellar hole. You will also encounter a nice stand of scruffy pitch

▲ Wilderness and Mount Monadnock in the distance, looking east from the summit of Mount Pisgah.

Needle tufts are distinctive on the trunk of this pitch pine. ▸

pine, with lots of needle tufts growing out of their trunks—an adaptation that allows them to stump sprout if portions of the trunk are killed by fire or if the tree is cut down.

On your return from the summit of Mount Pisgah, you will go left when you hit the connector trail, then right onto the Kilburn Loop Trail, and eventually back to Kilburn Road. Just before you get to the road, you have another choice to make. If you turn left on the John Summers Trail, you will be able to walk the perimeter of Kilburn Pond and even take a swim if you wish; this will add about a mile to your hike. Or you can cross Baker Brook and return to the road and your car.

If you decide to take the John Summers Trail, you will pass through sections that have old white pines and encounter a number of granite ledges on the shoreline; the ledges offer nice views of

This winter view of Kilburn Pond is close to the dam at its southern end. ▸

Kilburn Pond. The trail will wend away from the pond at two points, to go around bays on its eastern side. After going around the second bay, you will enter a stand of old-growth hemlocks. These trees are not large, generally less than 18 inches in diameter, but they have coarse bark plates and canopies with a lot of breakage. You will then cross two bridges—the second below the Kilburn Pond dam. Shortly after the second bridge, you will come back to the Kilburn Loop Trail. Take a right to get back to Kilburn Road. Like all the other foot trails on this outing, the John Summers Trail has a true wilderness feel about it until you come to the dam.

With regard to the homestead site's location, I believe the individual or family who lived there was from the Abenaki First Nation, and did not want to assimilate. The placement of the homestead miles from any others and close to the ledge with the view of Mount Monadnock is the basis for my hypothesis, because this was a sacred mountain for the Abenaki people. After I discovered the site, I asked a colleague interested in archaeology how I might confirm my belief. She advised me on how I could look for artifacts. Following her suggestions, I did find evidence of arrowhead points having been made on the site.

WANTASTIQUET MOUNTAIN

Remnants of wildfire along an old carriage road

DIFFICULTY	Moderate

LOCATION ▸ Across the Connecticut River from Brattleboro, Vermont

FEATURES FOCUS ▸ Basal fire scars, glacial impact, stump spouts

LENGTH	1 mile

A round-trip, uphill hike, this trail has an eroded section with some irregular footing. If you can visit in late April, the vernal wildflowers will be in bloom.

Rising 1000 feet above the Connecticut River across from Brattleboro, Vermont, New Hampshire's Wantastiquet Mountain is an icon throughout the region. I'll never forget my first visit to Brattleboro, during the summer of 1976. My wife and I were heading into downtown. As we approached Main Street, the road declined steeply and Wantastiquet rose dramatically in front of us. My wife simply said, "Wow!" as the mountain appeared above the river. Thanks to its location just a short walk from downtown Battleboro, Wantastiquet is a magnet for the residents of this Vermont city, as well as for people from farther afield. One of those visitors was Henry David Thoreau, who made the trip to Wantastiquet in 1856 to see its old, large trees (it was never cleared for agriculture). The mountain still retains many large trees, particularly its white pines.

Wantastiquet's vernal wildflowers are on full display in the spring. One of the best places to see wildflowers that like calcium-enriched soils is on a talus slope adjacent to the parking area, just off Route 119. In late April, a robust population of Dutchman's breeches, trout lilies, red trilliums, and wild ginger cover the talus slope. Another indicator of the enriched soils at this site is the presence of wild grape, with its vines covered in shaggy, brown bark. A large, 6-inch-diameter specimen grows right at the base of the talus slope.

Wild grape is one of our native plant species that can actually migrate through a forest. Grape plants do this by layering, sometimes growing over the canopies of their host trees and killing them. Eventually the dead tree falls over, and if the upper part of the grape-vine comes into contact with the soil, it can re-root at that point and in time disconnect from its original vine. In this way, wild grape can repeatedly hop through a forest. For that reason, in a forest like the one on Wantastiquet—never cleared for agriculture—it is not possible to know the true age of an individual wild grape.

You will be walking on the Summit Trail, an old carriage road constructed during the 1800s to allow easy access to the mountain's summit. Prior to the first switchback, look to the left for a large white pine that has a wound at its base. This wound is known as an uphill basal scar and is a strong indicator of previous wildfire. On a slope, leaves, branches, and logs are slowly pulled downhill by gravity, and every tree trunk stands in the way of this movement. A pile accumu-lates on the uphill side of an obstructing trunk, while its downhill side remains clear. If a fire is burning upslope, it runs past the clear downhill side of the tree, but when it hits the fuel pocket on the uphill side, it typically burns there long enough for the heat to kill the cam-bial tissue under the bark. After a number of years, the bark falls away, creating the uphill basal fire scar.

I chose Wantastiquet as an exploration because it has a long history of wildfires. In fact, I know of no better site to see evidence of fire in a New England forest. The most recent fires here were in 2007 and 2015. This walk will conclude within the site of the 2007 fire. As

▲ A large wild grapevine grows at the start of the Summit Trail.

▲ This basal scar on the uphill side of a white pine indicates a previous fire.

you continue up the trail, keep looking for uphill basal fire scars on the larger trees; they are quite common.

After you come around the second switchback on the road, look to your right, focusing on the variety of tree sizes there. You'll see scattered large white pines, then a lot of smaller multi-trunked trees, but no trees of intermediate size. This is known as age discontinuity and is more evidence of fire. The largest trees here are over 150 years of age. With their thick bark and a lot of thermal mass in their big trunks, these sizable trees can survive the heat of a fire. Trees with smaller trunks are killed outright, however. If the heat-killed trunks are hardwoods, they will stump sprout, creating multi-trunked trees. The ensuing forest then lacks trees of intermediate size.

You will soon come to a second gate, after which there is a rock outcropping on the left. Close to this outcrop are a few white pine snags that were killed by previous fires. The lower slope of the mountain has many such snags. A short walk up that outcrop provides a fine view down to Brattleboro on the far side of the river. You can also

▲ This example of age discontinuity was created by a fire that left smaller trees with multiple trunks and large white pines, but no trees of intermediate size.

A shagbark hickory stands next to a double-trunked white oak on Wantastiquet's southwest-facing slope.

look down on the island, to which the two Route 119 bridges are connected.

During the early 1800s, the island was much larger, at 22 acres. In 1862, a flood took the bulk of the island away, leaving just 8 acres. However, that was enough land to create Island Park, which opened to the public in 1911. The park featured a baseball field with a covered grandstand that could seat 1200 fans; a large pavilion that held dances, concert, plays, and bowling alleys; and an ice cream parlor. In 1927, the Connecticut River had its largest historical flood and Island Park was washed away, leaving the tiny remnant that remains today between the two bridges.

Climbing on the road above the rock outcrop, you will come to a section that has eroded down to the bedrock. Sections of the bedrock retain its glacial polish: a high sheen created by the silt and sand in the flowing ice that was dragged across the bedrock under great pressure. The bedrock in this section of the trail was covered in soil after the glacier's departure—protecting the polish from being pitted by lichen growth—until the soil eroded away relatively recently, in earth time. If you look downslope on the left side of the trail here, you will see a section of forest that has been spared by wildfire and supports a lot of hemlock—a species that is quite intolerant of fire.

After coming back to the intact carriage road, you will enter a section of forest dominated by white oak and shagbark hickory. This is a forest type that is rare in northern New England and far more characteristic of a state like Pennsylvania. Both white oak and shagbark hickory do well on the dry, warm sites that are typical of Wantastiquet's steep, southwest-facing slope. Shagbark is easily recognized by its very shaggy bark, which provides critical roosting places for endangered Indiana bats.

At the third switchback, look to the left for a north-headed carriage road that is no longer maintained. It can be seen as a raised,

⌃ Somewhat obscured by fallen leaves in this image, the start of an abandoned carriage road runs through the 2007 burn site.

⌃ On the edge of the 2007 fire site, there is a more open canopy and a denser understory of stump sprouts.

flat roadbed with troughs on each side. A short walk down this road will take you into the 2007 burn site. My guess is the road has been abandoned because of the number of fire-killed snags that have fallen across it.

When you reach the burn site, you will notice a big change in both the overstory and the understory of the forest. The overstory is much more open, while the understory is dense with hardwood stump sprouts. You will also see lots of standing and downed snags of trunks killed by the fire. A close examination shows that red oaks did far better surviving the blaze than the red maples, which were heavily impacted. Notice the vigorous regrowth of the mountain laurel, which has also resprouted following the burn.

More evidence of fire is the number of multi-trunked trees that have emerged from trees whose original trunks were not very big. Even if the original trunk has rotted away, its original size can be inferred by drawing a circle at ground level through the centers of the stump sprouts, because they emerged around the outside of the original trunk. Large trunks usually survive a fire, but small ones often don't, and if they are hardwoods, they stump sprout. A forest with a lot of multi-trunked trees whose original trunks were small

▴ This heat-killed, 4-inch red maple snag sent up stump sprouts.

▴ The carriage road leads up to the summit after the third switchback.

is strong evidence of fire, because small trees are rarely purposely cut in a forest.

Return to the carriage road and you will have a choice of either continuing on toward the summit or heading back down. At this point, you are only about a quarter of the way to the summit and have more than 2 miles remaining. However, the walk is on a graded carriage road that doesn't demand a lot of exertion, and the view from the top is quite nice.

VERMONT

AREA OF DETAIL

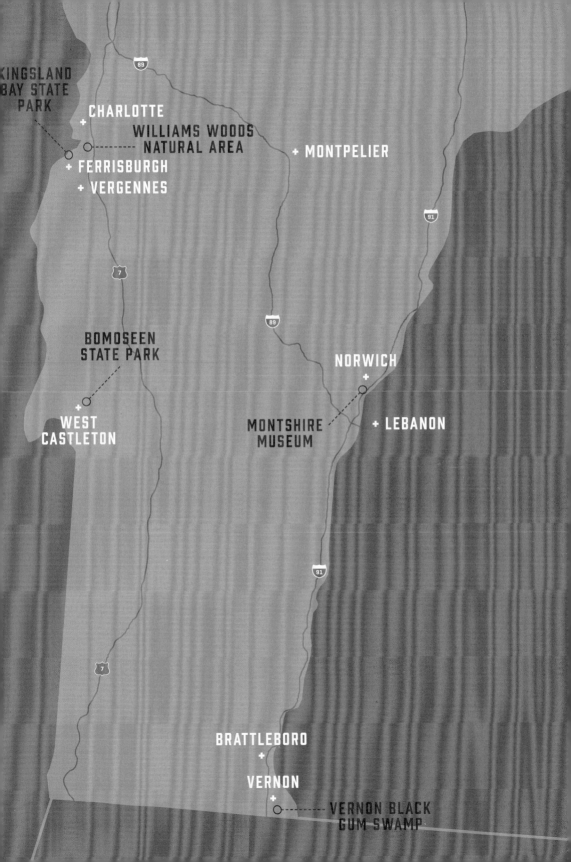

KINGSLAND
BAY STATE
PARK

+ CHARLOTTE

WILLIAMS WOODS
NATURAL AREA

+ MONTPELIER

+ FERRISBURGH
+ VERGENNES

7

BOMOSEEN
STATE PARK

NORWICH
+

MONTSHIRE
MUSEUM

+ LEBANON

+
WEST
CASTLETON

91

7

BRATTLEBORO
+

VERNON
+

VERNON BLACK
GUM SWAMP

KINGSLAND BAY STATE PARK

A peninsula walk featuring uncommon tree neighbors

DIFFICULTY
Easy

LOCATION ▸ Ferrisburgh, Vermont
FEATURES FOCUS ▸ Old growth, tree secrets: northern white cedar

LENGTH
.75 miles

This short, mostly level loop trail out to Macdonough Point and back is a gem, thanks to its lake views, calcium-enriched flora, unusual associations of trees, and scattered pockets of old-growth forest. In early May, the vernal wildflowers are in bloom.

Key to this unique ecosystem is its bedrock of dolomite—a form of limestone that is rich in calcium and magnesium. These two minerals are critical for creating rich soils; calcium in particular acts to buffer acidity that would leach away plant nutrients. The presence of plantain-leaved sedge near the start of the trail on the Kingsland Bay side of the point is evidence of the soil's calcium content. This plant doesn't resemble most sedges; its broad leaves form a basal rosette at ground level. Certain plants have very specific conditions in which they grow; such plants are known as eco-indicators. In this instance, the plantain-leaved sedge is an eco-indicator of calcium-enriched soils, with a pH around 7.

Associated with the sedge are a number of trees that also like soil endowed with calcium, including shagbark hickory, basswood, hop hornbeam, and northern white cedar. The hop hornbeam and shagbark hickory also like the drier soils that occur here as a result of the thin soil layer over the dolomite. As you continue down the trail, you will find there is a real diversity of tree species, including unusual associations

▴ Plantain-leaved sedge, with its broad, basal leaves, is an eco-indicator of the calcium-rich soil at Kingsland Bay State Park.

⏶ The trail travels over dolomite bedrock, here with a white ash on the left and a northern white cedar on the right.

⏶ Shagbark hickories like this serve as important roosts for endangered Indiana bats.

of poor- and rich-sited species growing together. There are areas with white ash growing with hemlock, and hemlock growing with Pennsylvania sedge. Usually this rich-sited sedge grows with hop hornbeam, shagbark hickory, and sugar maple, creating forest savannahs that have open understories with their ground covered in this grasslike sedge. I have never seen hemlock associating with white ash or Pennsylvania sedge. Farther on, red pine can be found growing with shagbark hickory—another first for me!

The large shags of the hickory's bark are critical summer roosting sites for bats, particularly the endangered Indiana bat. With its well-developed stands of shagbark hickory, this state park is an important bat research site in Vermont. This region of Lake Champlain also has the most northerly populations of shagbark hickory in the United States.

As you approach the point, keep an eye out for white pines that look advanced in age. These will be the first old-growth trees you will encounter and can be recognized by the horizontal fissures that separate their bark plates. If you look closely, you may notice that the bottom and top of each bark plate just above and below these fissures bumps out a bit. White pine trees generally don't develop this kind of scalloped, bark texture until they are at least 275 years of age. Although these trees are not that big, their bark tells us they have been here a long time. Because old-growth trees are scattered throughout the area, we can make an educated guess that Macdonough Point has always been forested and never open, agricultural land—most likely a result of its thin, rocky soils. A photo of the bark of an old-growth white pine can be seen in the chapter on Massachusetts's Monument Mountain.

At the end of the point, walking around, keep an eye on the right side of the trail for a number of northern white cedar trees with scars from lightning strikes. Whenever I encounter stands of this tree species on bluffs along the eastern shore of Lake Champlain, I see many hit by lightning. In fact, proportionally more northern white cedars display lightning scars than any other species, including trees that are quite a bit taller than cedars. You will see this same pattern here. Perhaps the northern white cedar is an especially strong conductor of electric charges. However, unlike white pine, I have never seen a cedar trunk blown completely apart from a steam explosion generated by a lightning strike (a result of internal sap being turned to steam by the lightning). Accordingly, all the cedar scars here seem to have resulted from bark only being blown off one side. Because lightning hits cedars frequently, remember to not to be out on a bluff like this during a thunderstorm. A lightning-scarred tree can be seen in the chapter on Tyler Mill Preserve in Connecticut.

Northern white cedars have a number of attractive qualities. They are not picky about growing conditions and can be found in widely diverse locations, including the dry and enriched limestone environment here. Northern white cedar is also the oldest-growing species in the northeastern states—individual trees have been dated at 1200 years. Although many of the cedars growing in this state park are not big, their tight trunk spirals indicate they are very old—as did the trunk spirals of the Atlantic white cedars in New Hampshire's Manchester Cedar Swamp. Northern white cedars also root graft with neighboring trees; if you spot one here growing in close proximity to another tree, see if they display any aboveground grafted roots. Finally, northern white cedar hollows from the inside out. Since its outer wood is rot resistant, hollow northern white cedar stumps can last more than 100 years.

I have been asked if I have a favorite tree species, and until about 5 years ago, I didn't. Then we bought a summer cottage in Down East Maine, where northern white cedar is common. After more than 60 years of admiring trees, this species has now become my favorite, in part because of its wide range of unique qualities.

Soon you will come to a ledge rising on your right, with lots of moss covering the dolomite. The calcium in this bedrock tends to be leached out by rainwater that is slightly acidic. As a result, the rock

These hollowed-out cedar stumps root grafted together before being cut many decades ago.

Dolomite outcrops such as this often support beds of moss.

Herb Robert grows in a bed of moss. It is an eco-indicator of soil rich in calcium.

A nice view of Camel's Hump in the distance over Lake Champlain.

develops pore spaces that can hold water for long periods of time, allowing the moss to better anchor itself. In some of these moss beds, you can find herb Robert growing. This is a delicate member of the geranium family that has finely divided leaves and small pink flowers. Like the plantain-leaved sedge, it is also an eco-indicator of thin, calcium-enriched soils.

After the dolomite ledge, you will come to a 3-way trail junction. Go right on the upper trail and climb a short rise. Watch for a low plant with leaves that have 3 round lobes. This is the round-lobed hepatica, another eco-indicator of enriched, thin soils. It flowers in April and has blooms that range from white to violet. The flowers track the sun through the day, always facing directly toward it. On cold days, insects will land on the flowers to warm themselves in the direct sunlight hitting the blossoms—a clever trick of the plant to spur pollination.

After you climb the rise and pass a picnic table, you will come to a nice view of Camel's Hump across the lake. A short distance farther, there will be an old-growth red oak on the right with a completely healed lightning scar on its trunk, then two old-growth sugar maples. At this point, the forest abruptly changes to a much younger stand of mixed hemlock. After another 600 feet or so, you are once again in old-growth specimens of red oak and sugar maple. Eventually you will emerge from the woods and can finish your loop, or you can take a left and hike the lower trail, which goes up and over the bluffs along the lakeshore, with lots of cliffside cedars. This lower trail is a bit rougher going.

WILLIAMS WOODS NATURAL AREA

Ancient sea bed supports rare ecosystem

DIFFICULTY
Moderate

LOCATION ▸ Charlotte, Vermont
FEATURES FOCUS ▸ Glacial impact, pillows and cradles, stone walls and early agriculture, white pine weevil

LENGTH
1.25 miles

Level and a bit over a mile in length, this trail includes many sections of easily negotiated 2-plank boardwalk. However, there are also parts of the trail with exposed roots that can catch shoes and boots. Roadside parking is limited.

Williams Woods is a remnant of what is known as a clay-plain forest. This extensive forest used to surround Lake Champlain, before European settlement. The clay was deposited as glacial outwash flowed into the Champlain Sea, when the ancient Laurentide Ice Sheet was receding back into what is now Quebec (15,000 to 17,000 years ago). The Champlain Sea covered a large portion of present-day Quebec, Ontario, and a section stretching southward into New York and Vermont. In the Features Focus chapter, I mentioned how the weight of the glacial ice—which was over a mile thick—pushed the continental crust hundreds of feet down, into the mantle of the earth. In areas that had been clear of the ice for a couple thousand years, the crust rebounded and rose hundreds of feet out of the mantle, while areas just around the melting glacier were far lower. Here, the area around the melting glacier was flooded by the Atlantic Ocean as the ice sheet retreated northward.

Meltwater rivers flowing into the Champlain Sea first deposited sand, forming deltas where the rivers entered. However, the fine silts and clays were carried out into the sea, slowly settling to form its floor. In time, the crust in the Champlain Valley rebounded and seawater drained out of the basin. This eventually left a much smaller

Lake Champlain and a surrounding clay plain—the now-exposed
floor of the Champlain Sea.

Because the soils of the clay plain were free of rocks and fertile,
they were quickly converted to farm fields in the 18th and 19th
centuries, in time leaving less than 1 percent of the original clay-
plain forest. This is why The Nature Conservancy has protected this
forest; it is now a rare ecosystem with a number of oak and hickory
species, plus white ash and red maple. One of the oaks—bur oak—is
an uncommon tree for New England.

Bur oak is a tree that is mostly found from the lake states to
the Dakotas and down into eastern Texas. There are three disjunct
populations of bur oak in New England—one in central Maine, one on
the very western boundary of Massachusetts and Connecticut, and
one in the Champlain Basin of Vermont. The two western-most New
England populations are restricted to clay-plain forests.

Beginning the exploration, you will be on many sections of
boardwalk because clay-plain soil is wet. As you enter a young mixed
forest, notice the high number of downed trees. Because the soils
in a clay plain are dense and lack good aeration, the roots of trees

A distinctive
triple-trunked red
maple can be seen
just before the
trail's first stream
crossing. ▸

are very surficial, which makes them more prone to being toppled by wind than trees in glacial-till soils. You will also encounter sections of the trail covered in tree roots because of their surficial nature. However, the soils of the clay plain are very productive for tree growth. This is visible in the sizable red maples growing here. Not far in on the right side of the trail is a red maple with a trunk diameter of about 30 inches and a burl on one of its roots. This is an unusually large red maple, yet it probably is not that old. A bit farther on, look for a large, triple-trunked red maple on the right, before you come to the first stream crossing.

After you cross the stream, keep an eye to the left of the trail for some large white oaks. Both white oak and swamp white oak grow in Williams Woods. These two oaks can be differentiated by their leaves. White oak leaves are deeply notched, while swamp white oak leaves are more filled out, notched less deeply, and look more like those of a chestnut oak. Similar to bur oak, swamp white oak is only found in Vermont on the clay-plain soils of the Champlain Basin. The white oaks, swamp white oaks, and bur oaks all reach close to 300 years of age in the Williams Woods and are impressive specimens.

Soon you will make your second stream crossing and come to a junction with the loop portion of the trail. Take a right and do the loop in a counterclockwise fashion. Keep an eye out on the left for a hemlock that has a lightning scar on its trunk, with a number of woodpecker holes excavated in the scar. The callus growing over the scar shows that the strike happened many decades ago. The trail then passes a number of old white pines with large bark plates. At one point the trail passes right between two of these old pines. A little farther along, the forest becomes much younger, with root-covered sections where the footing is more challenging. In time the trail will be adjacent to a wetland. On the right at the wetland-forest interface is an impressive bur oak. The bark on older bur oaks such as this one tends to be more distinctly ridged than on white or swamp white oaks. At this point, the trail will turn to the left, cross an ephemeral drainage, and pass an old, open-grown hemlock on the right with large, low branches.

This tree grew by itself in the open. Trees like this hemlock usually indicate a former pasture, where trees were left to provide

▲ An old, open-grown hemlock like this was by itself in the open as it grew, as evidenced by its large, low branches.

shade for livestock in summer. However, a close look at the ground shows that it is smooth and even, completely lacking pillows and cradles (the pits and mounds caused by the root masses of toppled trees). We can deduce that this section of the Williams Woods was once plowed, removing the pillows and cradles that are frequent just before this section of the trail. This area was plowed initially to create either a crop field or a hayfield, then possibly converted to a pasture before being abandoned.

After passing the old hemlock, you will enter a young, white pine–dominated stand with weevil-hit trees that are between 40 and 50 years old. Based on the age of these weevil-hit pines, this part of Williams Woods was agricultural land abandoned during the 1970s. You'll proceed through this abandoned farmland for a good distance before entering an older white pine stand. Once in this stand, keep looking to the right for a number of downed pines. When downed trees lie in the same direction like this, it is evidence of a blowdown. It takes about 20 years for downed pines to drop their bark and for moss to cover the trunks, as has happened here. The winds from this blowdown came from the northeast, evidence of a hurricane whose track was to the east of Williams Woods and that hit sometime in the 1990s. The only hurricane to impact this part of Vermont in the 1990s was Hurricane Floyd, which occurred in September 1999. As you continue on the trail, you will come to tip-ups (uprooted base and root masses) from downed trees, in which the clay is clearly visible as part of their root systems. This dense clay, and the shallow roots it causes, is the reason the trees here are so vulnerable to being blown over.

After the blowdown, you will enter what I consider the most interesting part of Williams Woods. Here you will see scattered old

▲ Downed trees are remnants of Hurricane Floyd, which hit this site in 1999.

▲ A tip-up from a downed pine clearly shows the dense clay soils of this woodland, as well as the shallow roots that clay produces.

bur oaks and basswoods with an understory of much younger hemlocks. If you examine the canopies of these bur oaks, you will notice they have a lot of character, from wind and ice storms breaking branches over the centuries they have existed here. The bur oaks can be identified by their noticeably ridged bark.

What is intriguing about this section of the forest is that it has distinct age discontinuity. There are scattered large, old bur oaks, then an understory of much younger hemlock, but no trees of intermediate age or stature. When a forest has trees over 150 years old and age discontinuity like this, it is usually evidence of a previous wildfire. The largest trees survived the fire and everything else was killed and replaced by younger saplings and stump sprouts that grew following the blaze. But there is no evidence of fire in this section of the woods. With a lack of stumps or multi-trunked trees, there is also no evidence of logging here. Perhaps the best explanation for the age discontinuity is that this area was once an older woodland, with forest-grown bur oaks. It may have then been opened for pasture, leaving scattered oaks for shade trees. It's also possible it was abandoned 50 to 70 years ago, allowing hemlock to colonize the understory. This is a rather unique situation, because all the pasture trees I encounter are open grown, with large, low limbs—not forest-grown trees like these bur oaks. The forest structure in this

▲ This old bur oak has classic, characteristic ridged bark.

▲ Host-specific pleasing fungus beetles feed and mate on the host-specific *Ganoderma tsugae*. An interrelated, host-specific twofer!

▲ An excellent example of an aboveground root graft between two hemlocks.

part of Williams Woods is quite unusual—exactly why I think it is the highlight of this exploration.

Also in this section of the woods is a downed hemlock whose trunk supports lots of *Ganoderma tsugae*: a host-specific shelf fungus with a shiny lacquer-like top. *Ganoderma tsugae* only grows on dead hemlocks. On a visit in June, these fungal fruiting bodies were covered with pleasing fungus beetles—a striking species that is glossy black with bold orange bands. These beetles foraging and mating on the fungus make quite a sight. Never having encountered this species of beetle before, I stood for many minutes, mesmerized. Since this insect is host-specific to *Ganoderma tsugae* and only feeds on this species of fungus, it was also my first encounter with an interrelationship between two host-specific species! The beetle only eats a fungus that only consumes dead hemlock.

Moving through these bur oaks, watch on the left for a big red maple whose bark looks more like that of a white oak. It is directly adjacent to the trail. This tree has an open wound, and if you look into it, you will see that the trunk is hollow. Directly across the trail from this maple are two hemlocks whose aboveground roots have clearly grafted together. Here you can easily see a root graft that allows these two trees to share energy, nutrients, and even information.

When you have completed the loop, turn right to cross the stream. About 100 feet after your second stream crossing, look to the right side of the trail for a large, old red maple whose bark is shaggy. It is similar to that of a shagbark hickory, however, the shags of a red maple are neither as broad nor long as a shagbark. This is one way you can distinguish red maple from sugar maple—by their bark. Red maples, as they age, create strips of bark that curl away from the trunk at their tops and bottoms. Sugar maple trees also have strips of bark, but most of the strips stay attached at the top and bottom. On one side, though, sugar maple bark does curl away from the trunk.

From here it is a quick walk back to the road.

◄ The bark of an old red maple is similar to shagbark hickory.

BOMOSEEN STATE PARK

DIFFICULTY
Moderate

Ecosystems supported in both rich and poor soils

LENGTH
1.5 miles

LOCATION ▸ West Castleton, Vermont
FEATURES FOCUS ▸ Beech bark scale, old growth, stone walls and early agriculture, white pine weevil

Bomoseen Loop Trail will take you through a number of different forest communities based on changes in soils and varied histories. It is accessed at the southern end of the state park, provides good footing, and has an elevation gain of about 300 feet.

The lower woodlands are calcium enriched, supporting lots of shagbark hickory, sugar maple, white oak, and Pennsylvania sedge. The upper woodlands have soils poorer in nutrients and are dominated by red oak and hemlock. This difference in soil quality is also related to past agricultural use; the lower areas are former crop fields and pastures, while the upper areas were left as woodlots.

The trail begins just past the ranger station, crosses the road that goes down to the shore of Lake Bomoseen, then comes to a stone wall at the bottom of a wildflower meadow. A close look at the wall will show that it is composed of many small stones, indicating that the wildflower meadow was once a crop field. Looking at the ground on the uphill side of the stone wall, notice that it is almost 2 feet higher than the ground on the downhill side of the wall. You may also notice that the ground on the uphill side is level for about 10 feet before it rises uphill in the meadow. This level feature is called a bottom-plow terrace. Farmers plowed across a hill's slope and pushed the plow furrow downslope, because it was less work than pushing it upslope. Each year, soil moved down the slope, and where the plowing stopped near the stone fence, it was deposited in the accumulating terrace on the uphill side of the wall. A terrace of this size means the crop field was worked for many decades.

Climb the slope of the meadow and you will start to get limited views of Lake Bomoseen. Near the top of the meadow is the loop portion of the trail; go left and walk the trail in a clockwise fashion. As you leave the meadow and enter a young woodland, observe that the ground, though sloping, has a smooth and even surface from all the plowing when it was a crop field. Upslope is an older forest separated from the younger one by a barbed wire fence. Barbed wire fencing replaced stone walls in the 1870s and was used to keep livestock in pastures and out of hayfields and crop fields. This means that the older upslope forest was a pasture when it was abandoned to grow back to forest. There is also a line of older sugar maples that runs along the boundary of the pasture and crop field—these were no doubt left for collecting sap to make maple syrup.

Soon the trail crosses into the former pasture, where you will find lots of shagbark hickories and grape vines, indicating a calcium-enriched soil. There are some weevil-hit white pines on the left side of the trail that grew in the open while the pasture was still being

▲ The wildflower meadow offers a peek of Lake Bomoseen.

Shagbark hickories indicate calcium-enriched soils.

Large, low limbs and more than two trunks above where it splits are clues that this white pine was both open grown and hit by weevils.

used. This can be discerned by their large, low limbs and also that they support more than two trunks once they split. White pines that colonize a site after abandonment form dense stands, where they quickly grow upward without large, low branches. If hit by the weevil, they support two trunks above the fork. Continuing on, you will come to a savannah composed of Pennsylvania sedge and white oak. The ground here is covered in sedge, making it look somewhat like a woodland lawn.

You will soon leave the abandoned pasture and enter an older forest that was never cleared and left as a woodlot. In this stand, you will see an old, forest-grown white oak on the left, and, when the trail levels out, another old white pine on the right. Also significant is that there are no weevil-hit pines, meaning that they all grew up in a forest setting.

Eventually the forest will become dominated by hemlock and red oak, indicating you have entered the area with poorer soil. Many of the oaks here are multi-trunked, suggesting they were logged in the past. Based on the size of their coppiced trunks, they were cut

▲ A beautiful, old, forest-grown white oak.

▲ This beech tree is infected by scale insects, seen here as small white dots and marks on the bark.

back in the early 1900s. By creating a circle through the middles of the coppiced trunks at ground level you can estimate the diameter of the original trunk that was cut. A little farther, the forest will shift to predominantly beech and red oak. On one section of the trail you will enter what is known as a beech hell, an area caused by beech bark scale disease.

The scale insect lives on the bark and feeds on beech tree sap. The insects appear as little white dots on the bark of beech trees and compromise the tree's bark, allowing *Neonectria* fungi to invade. These fungi weaken the beech tree's trunk, which in turn often snaps off, killing the aboveground portion of the tree, but not its root system. As the trunk dies, it is replaced by a dense clone of root sprouts. After a number of outbreaks, the beech trees in a stand become replaced by a dense understory of root sprouts. These form the beech hell.

After passing through the beech hell, you will start to descend and come back to calcium-enriched soils. Look for an outcrop covered in lush mats of moss; the moss indicates that this bedrock has a good amount of calcium in it. As the calcium is leached out it, it creates

▲ This black birch tree germinated and grew on a white pine nurse stump. When the stump decays, the stilted roots will stay as they are aboveground.

▲ A well-developed Pennsylvania sedge savannah, with shagbark hickory and white oak.

pores that hold moisture and help the moss anchor itself to the bedrock. Another indicator that you have reentered an area of enriched soil is the presence of basswood—an eco-indicator of a nutrient-rich site.

Farther on, you will enter a well-developed Pennsylvania sedge savannah with shagbark hickory and white oak. Just as you come to this site, look to the right to see a black birch growing on a white pine nurse stump. This black birch germinated in the center of the white pine stump and its roots grew down just under the bark before the bark was shed from the stump. In time, the stump will disappear, leaving this stilted-root birch. Stilted-root trees can also grow from nurse logs; in this case the log rots away, and the aboveground roots are left visible. In New England, white pine and spruce most commonly serve as nurse stumps and nurse logs. Both decay slowly from the outside, giving ample time for small-seeded, shade-tolerant trees like black birch, yellow birch, and hemlock to establish.

Here I found some red oak leaves lying on the ground and took a photo of them. In the accompanying image, a large leaf lies next to a smaller one. Both of these leaves probably came off the same tree, because all oaks have dimorphic leaves—two different kinds of leaves. In this case, one of the leaves is a sun leaf and the other a shade leaf. Which do you think is the sun leaf? If you chose the small one, you are correct. Sun leaves occur at the very top of an oak's canopy and are exposed to direct sunlight. They are small in size, have deeper notches in their leaves, and also have a thicker cuticle covering the leaf, making the sun leaves feel more leathery. Their small size and heavy cuticle are to protect sun leaves from loss of moisture. The deep notches allow maximum light to get to the interior shade leaves, which can do a lot of photosynthesis without moisture loss. In this way, the sun leaves are creating a microenvironment for the shade leaves, allowing oaks to do more photosynthesis than all other regional, broad-leaved trees on dry sites.

If an ice storm breaks apart the canopy of a red oak, and a branch that was previously in the shade is suddenly exposed to full sunlight, the following spring the branch will still put forth shade leaves—because those leaves were preformed during the prior growing season. However, the year after that, the branch will produce sun leaves. This is an example of the oak's biological cognizance—the ability of an organism to receive cues from its environment and then respond correctly to those cues.

Continuing your descent back to the meadow, look to the right for a white pine that has large, low limbs growing on one side of its trunk. This is what I call a border tree, meaning that it grew on the edge of a forest that bordered an open area. Because of the pine's biological cognizance, it sensed a lot of light on its open side and put forth limbs there to take advantage of the light, while on its side shaded by the forest, no limbs were produced. In fact, trees most likely have a greater awareness of light than we do, with three times more kinds of light sensors than humans—an interesting fact to consider as you transition from the shade of the forest to the radiant light of the meadow.

▴ A shade and sun leaf from a red oak. The sun leaf on the right is smaller, with deeper notches, to allow sun to reach the interior shade leaf, on the left, which has more surface area and is a photosynthesis champ.

▴ A border white pine with large, low limbs growing on the side that once faced open farmland.

MONTSHIRE MUSEUM

Sleuthing important events in a forest's previous life

DIFFICULTY
Easy

LENGTH
1 mile

LOCATION ▸ Norwich, Vermont
FEATURES FOCUS ▸ Basal fire scars, Great NE Hurricane of 1938, pillows and cradles, tipped trees

Be sure to check in at the front desk for any fees. The trail is mostly level with good footing.

This exploration of the Montshire Museum's enriched woodlands has a nice array of forest types, mostly related to a unique variety of disturbance histories. The walk follows the Ridge Trail (with blue blazes); you'll find the trailhead about 100 meters up the road above the parking lot. It begins with an uphill climb then levels off just after the forest temperature kiosk to the right of the trail.

Note ledge outcroppings on the right. Just after the second outcropping, as the trail descends, look upslope for a number of trees that have been tipped—their trunks are lying at an acute angle to the ground for a number of feet before taking a sharp turn and growing straight upward. These were young trees tipped by strong winds. The vertical trunk was the lowest living limb on the tree when it was tipped. This limb then became the new trunk, while the rest of the original trunk above this limb died and decayed away. Only small trees, with trunks usually less than 6 inches in diameter, remain tipped like this. Larger trees get tipped as well, but as they are pushed by the wind, they develop so much momentum that they crash to the ground. Because all these trees got tipped to the northwest, the winds came from the southeast—the result of the Great New England Hurricane of 1938 that hit this forest around 7 p.m., September 21. Nearly 700 people were lost along the New England seaboard.

◄ This red maple was tipped to the northwest by a 1938 hurricane.

The trail proceeds a bit farther before turning to the left and crossing a bridge. At the Life on Bark Exhibit post, look about 40 feet downslope from the trail and you can see three hemlocks that have uphill basal scars—the result of a past fire. These scars originated when forest debris—dead leaves, twigs, organic material—fell down the hill over time and was stopped by the trees, accumulating on the trunks' uphill sides. The fire lingered on these piles of gathered dry material on the uphill side. The heat killed the cambial tissue under the bark and the bark later fell away.

A careful examination of this site will also reveal charcoal. Behind the red oak at the Life on Bark Exhibit post is a large pillow and cradle created by a fallen tree's root mass, with the decaying downed trunk of the tree still present. This tree was dropped by a thunderstorm in the first half of the 20th century. Charcoal created by the ensuing fire can be found on this fallen trunk.

Just beyond where the trail passes between two red oaks, more charcoal can be found in the soil on the right side of the trail. This fire was a small one, probably accidentally started by someone working in the woods many decades ago based on the amount of callus that has grown over the nearby hemlocks' basal scars.

When I walked this trail, it was a mast year for the red oaks. Acorns were everywhere; it was sort of like walking on marbles. All our trees with cones or large seeds—such as pine, red oak, hickory, beech—mast, which is a process in which all the trees of a certain species over a large area limit seed production for a number of years in a row. During that time, they store the energy that could have gone into seed production as starch in their roots. Then, during a mast year, they all mobilize that energy and bring forth a huge crop of seeds. A few years ago, red oaks from Down East Maine to the Hudson Valley were all masting, covering almost all of New England.

If you think about it, masting is a gamble for an individual tree. Let's say a red oak has been storing energy for five years. Then, the winter before the mast year, the tree gets its canopy ripped apart by an ice storm or taken down by wind. So much reproductive potential, wasted. Why not just produce acorns every year? The answer is not what you may think.

Many people believe masting oaks are trying to thwart gray squirrels. In point of fact, gray squirrels *help* the oaks by dispersing and burying acorns, which dramatically improves establishment rates of the large seeds. The real problem that masting addresses for oaks is the acorn weevil. I have never seen an acorn weevil in the wild, because it is a small insect that stays in the canopy of oak trees. During summer, when acorns are forming, female weevils lay one egg in each acorn they find on the tree. The weevil larvae then hatch and start eating the meat of the acorn, eventually destroying the seed's viability. So if all the oaks suppress acorn production for a few years, they depress the weevil population and then completely overwhelm them during a mast year. It is such a successful strategy that if you see an oak, the odds are 99 percent it was spawned in a mast year. When gray squirrels pick up an acorn they give it a little shake. In this way, they can tell if an acorn has been compromised by a weevil. If it is, they simply drop it. The only acorns squirrels bury are plump, healthy ones.

Obviously, trees that mast are in communication to time the mast year, most likely using airborne chemicals released from their leaves so that populations on opposite sides of rivers or on islands get the message.

As you continue down the trail, you will find subtle pillows and cradles, evidence of a former pasture—versus a crop field, in which the ground would have been plowed to remove the mounds and pits.

However, when you approach the large coppiced red oak with the Bird's Eye View platform, you will have left the former pasture.
Just before this coppiced red oak, on the
left side of the trail, you will find a large pillow with a triple-trunked paper birch growing on it. Based on the size of the birch's
trunks, they are in the range of 75 to 100
years old, meaning the original birch was
cut in the early 1900s. By making a circle
through the centers of these three trunks
at ground level, we can assume the original

▲ This triple-trunked paper birch germinated on a
pillow formed by a tree that was downed in the late
1700s or early 1800s.

tree was about 2 feet in diameter and about 100 years old when cut.
Since the birch has no stilted roots, it germinated after the roots of
the downed tree completely decayed away and made a pillow. For a
pillow of this size to form, it would take about 40 years. Adding all
these years together, we get a range of 215–240 years, meaning the
thunderstorm that produced this pillow, and others like it in this area,
occurred between 1779 and 1804. We can tell it was a thunderstorm
because the wind that created these large pillows and cradles came
out of the west, and from that direction, only thunderstoms create
winds that can topple trees. All of this indicates we are in a section of
the forest that has always been wooded, because the first agricultural
lands were not abandoned in New England until the 1840s.

This is also confirmed by the Bird's Eye View red oak. Its four
coppiced trunks are at least 75 years old, meaning the original oak
was cut around World War II or earlier—possibly during the same
logging that cut the birch. The original trunk was at least 3 feet in
diameter and well over 100 years of age. Doing the math again, that
means this oak's acorn germinated before 1840. Another confirma-
tion that this site has always been forested can be seen at the post
for the Mossy Outcrop Exhibit. On the right side of the trail are the
remains of two very large white pine stumps, one of which is a nurse
stump for a hemlock. Both of these white pines were 4 feet in diameter and at that size, at least 150 years old. The amount of decay in
the stumps suggest they were cut around 100 years ago. That math
means these trees germinated in the time of the Revolutionary War,
or earlier, possibly in the same mast year.

clockwise from left A coppiced red oak supports the Bird's Eye View platform. • Only a decayed stump remains of a large white pine. • This hemlock grew from a white pine nurse stump. The pine was cut at the same time as the decayed one nearby.

It is worth taking the short side trail to the Mossy Outcrop, a calcium-enriched phyllitic schist completely covered in ferns and moss. The bedrock of the eastern border of Vermont is phyllitic schist—a low-grade metamorphic rock that formed under a bit more heat and pressure than slate, and as such, lost its flat, smooth surface. The schist formed over 400 million years ago and was derived from fine ocean sediments. During some periods, the fine sediments had a good amount of calcium deposited with them and at other times, not as much calcium. Calcium-enriched phyllite usually supports a lot of moss, while calcium-poor phyllite doesn't and has a sheen similar to slate.

Continuing on the trail, you will come back into former pasture, with smaller pillows and cradles; however, keep an eye on the right side of the trail for a very large pillow and cradle right below a ledge. This is probably the largest pillow and cradle I have ever encountered in New England. From the bottom of the cradle to the top of the

▲ The Mossy Outcrop is composed of calcium-enriched phyllitic schist, which encourages moss accumulation.

▲ Smooth, even ground such as this indicates previous agricultural plowing and lacks pillows and cradles.

▲ Plantain-leaved sedge and maidenhair fern (to the right) are eco-indicators of enriched soil.

▲ A quarry where the metamorphic rock phyllite was once extracted.

pillow is about 5 feet. After this feature, you will come to the Wood Frog Pool post, where the Ridge Trail descends to the left. After the trail goes over a small ledge, look to the right for a pocket of maidenhair fern and blue cohosh. These two species are strong eco-indicators for enriched soils that have a pH of 7 or higher.

Next you will cross a bridge and come to a younger forest that lacks pillows and cradles and has smooth, even ground from past plowing as a crop field or hayfield. As the trail levels out you will be in a young stand of bitternut hickory with Pennsylvania sedge, again indicating rich soils. This field was most likely abandoned when the museum acquired the land in 1989.

Back at the parking lot, it is worthwhile, particularly if you are there in early May, to take the Woodland Garden Trail, where many vernal ephemeral wildflowers will be in spring bloom. These include spring beauties, Dutchman's breeches, squirrel corn, wild leeks, and trout lilies. All of these wildflowers grow up in April and do all their photosynthesis when the forest canopy has no leaves. Then in May, they die back as other woodland wildflowers like blue cohosh and baneberry start to grow. In this way, these two groups of species temporally separate their growth niches so they don't compete for light. As a result of this niche separation, the herbaceous understory of our enriched woodlands is exceptionally diverse.

Along this trail is also a site where phyllite—the metamorphic rock similar to slate—was quarried, next to a footbridge. I do not know if this quarry was supplying rock for building material or if it was for the calcium-enriched rock to make lime when Europeans first settled here.

VERNON BLACK GUM SWAMP

Rare old-growth chestnut; a swamp unchanged in 1000 years

LOCATION ▸ Vernon, Vermont
FEATURES FOCUS ▸ Chestnut blight, Great NE Hurricane of 1938, tree secrets: black gum, stump sprouts, tipped trees

DIFFICULTY
Moderate

LENGTH
.75 miles

T his short loop trail provides good footing; there is one short section across an outcrop. The moderate rating is due to a steep uphill climb to the swamp that is about 600 feet long. During wet periods, sections of the trail adjacent to the swamp may be wet. Please do not walk in the swamp unless there is a decent snow cover. It is a very fragile ecosystem and walking on the hummocks will negatively impact vegetation. The best time to go is in early to mid-October, when the black gum (also known as tupelo) is at peak foliage.

This swamp is part of the J. Maynard Miller Municipal Forest in the town of Vernon, Vermont. It has two quite impressive features: a primeval old-growth swamp with trees exceeding 500 years of age, and evidence of a former old-growth stand of American chestnut— the only such evidence I have encountered in New England. Sadly, the evidence of the large, old-growth chestnut stumps is decaying away; within a decade or so it will no longer be visible.

Black gum is a southern swamp tree, though it does extend into our region. Here and throughout the northern portions of New England, black gum swamps are surprisingly found on the tops of ridges, despite the high winds typically found in such locations. Why? The species has adapted to survive strong winds. Its wood is very brittle, and it rots easily, so many black gums have hollow trunks. When hit by high winds, the tops of these trees snap off, leaving a portion of their trunk standing. The black gum is also able to resprout new limbs below broken areas. So when heavy winds buffet ridgetop swamps such as the one here in Vernon, black gum trees are able to withstand the onslaught, while our other species of swamp trees are toppled.

Begin the trail at the kiosk and make a moderate climb to a woods road. When you reach the road, turn left and follow the red-blazed trail in a clockwise fashion. Cross a small, ephemeral flowage (wet area) and then start your steeper uphill ascent to the swamp.

When you reach the swamp, you will see that many of the large black gums have trunks that rise about 40 feet and abruptly stop at a point where a mass of horizontal branches now grow. This last breakage event happened when the Great New England Hurricane of 1938 blew down all the other trees and left the black gum trunks broken but standing. One dramatic example can be seen at the point where the trail skirts the very edge of the swamp. This black gum's trunk displays many breakage events, each depicted where the trunk makes an abrupt turn, called an elbow. Here you will also be able to see the oldest black gum in the area, about 50 feet out in the swamp. You can identify it by the very coarse bark on the right side of its trunk.

▲ A contorted black gum's elbows show where the trunk has broken multiple times in its life.

Because these trees can survive repeated wind events, and hollow out so they aren't logged, they can reach great ages. In this swamp, the oldest trees well exceed 500 years. In New England, the oldest black gums are close to 700 years old. That is almost twice the age of the region's other old-growth species—quite an accomplishment.

Another notable feature of the black gum is its bark and the distinct differences in bark texture on various portions of the trunk. On many of the older trees, some of the fissures between bark plates are a good 4 inches deep, while on other sides of their trunks there are hardly any fissures at all. Close examination shows that the deep fissures always occur on sides of the trunk that are leaning toward the ground, while smoother bark occurs on trunk portions facing the sky. Why would this be? The bark of the black gum exfoliates easily. Skyward-facing surfaces capture wet snow. When it freezes and expands, the bark plates are exfoliated, while ground-facing portions are protected and develop a bark truly characteristic of the tree's age.

▲ The bark of this black gum has coarse plates on the right, smoother bark on the left.

The Vernon black gum swamp has limited vascular plant diversity, with just five species of trees, two species of shrubs, two species of ferns, and a handful of wildflower species. However, the swamp's appeal is in its primeval appearance. How it looks today is likely just how it looked over 1000 years ago. In a region with such a dramatic disturbance regime—from frequent blowdowns, logging, and wildfires, to wet snow and icing events—finding an ecosystem that has maintained its struc-ture and composition for a millennium is truly extraordinary!

A good time to visit this swamp is in the latter part of June, when the black gum blooms. Its flowers produce a large quan-tity of nectar and are highly sought after by bees, as referenced in the song by Van Morrison, "Tupelo Honey." Because the black gums readily hollow out, honeybees often develop hives in their trunks. When

▲ The remains of an American chestnut tree that was cut twice and had four trunks. A few of the 1-foot-diameter coppiced stumps can still be seen.

trees are flowering, the canopy of the black gum swamp is literally abuzz with the sound of thousands of bees. Another great time to visit the swamp is in early October, when its crimson leaves dapple the emerald-green of the sphagnum moss.

Reaching the northwestern end of the swamp, you will encoun-ter the sole black gum that was blown down by the 1938 hurricane. As you move around the end of the swamp to its northeastern side, you will come to the Delmarre Divide Trail, blazed in blue on your left. Forty feet after this junction, keep an eye peeled for a large, moss-covered mound on the right side of the trail. This is what's left of an American chestnut stump that was about 5 feet in diameter at ground level. Another 150 feet farther, you will come to another chestnut stump, again on the right side, which had four trunks, each roughly 1 foot in diameter. The one with four trunks was first cut around 1875, causing the stump to sprout new trunks. These four trunks were subsequently salvaged due to chestnut blight in a second 1915 cutting, when the stump-sprouted trunks were 40 years old.

American chestnut is one of northern New England's three rot-resistant hardwood trees with stumps that naturally hollow out as they decay. These stumps can be visible for over a century. The other two species are white oak and black locust.

Chestnut blight has had a devastating impact on the ecology of North America's eastern temperate deciduous forest. The blight was accidentally introduced by imported trees around 1900, and was deadly to the American chestnut—previously one of the most common forest trees in the eastern United States. These trees had trunks up to 14 feet in diameter and produced the most consumed nut in North America. But in only 30 years, it was almost completely eradicated by the blight.

I first discovered this site on the northeastern side of the swamp in 1978. Many years later, I realized I had happened upon one of the most unique forests in all of New England. In 1978, coppiced chestnut stumps were everywhere. Now less than a dozen remain— the others having succumbed to decay and appearing simply as moss-covered mounds. By drawing a circle through the center of all those coppiced stumps cut in 1915, I found that the original trees cut in 1875 ranged from 3 to 6 feet in diameter at ground level. That implied this had been an old-growth stand of American chestnut, with trees possibly exceeding 300 years of age. In my 40-plus years wandering the forests of the Northeast, I have never encountered another site with evidence of an old-growth chestnut forest. Coupled with the adjacent black gum swamp, this place is truly exceptional. Sadly, in another few decades the unique history of this site will no longer be visible.

I believe there is hope for the American chestnut, though. I have encountered five stands of American chestnuts that display resistance and are reproducing with seedlings and saplings in the understory. Each new generation should have greater resistance than their predecessors. Hopefully, they will coevolve with the fungus to the point that they can survive.

Moving down the trail on the northeastern side of the swamp, you will come to a junction with the Footbridge Trail. At this point, on the left side of the red-blazed trail, there is a white pine that was hit by lightning and can be identified by the spiral-shaped scar on its trunk. To clearly see the full extent of this scar, you will need to leave the trail.

All trees are genetically determined to have wood grains that grow in a spiral pattern—a pattern that is usually hidden by the bark. This is part of a tree's phyllotaxy and causes each tier of branches to be offset from the one below it as a means to reduce shading. By my count, 90 percent of trees, regardless of species, spiral to the right as one looks up the trunk; 10 percent spiral left. This is very much like right- and left-handedness in people. However, the intensity of the spiral is environmentally determined. If trees elongate their trunks quickly, like pulling on a spring, the tightness of the spiral is reduced. Yet any tree that does not stretch out quickly—due to wind stunting, canopy suppression, or other reasons—develops more intense spirals. Lightning strikes follow a tree's wood grain pattern, often creating spiral scars.

There's an old adage that lightning never strikes in the same place twice. A close look at the top of this white pine's spiral scar will confirm that this adage is wrong. This pine has been hit twice in the exact same spot by lightning. The most recent strike, in 2016, blew out pieces of the trunk's wood. The previous strike, from the late 1990s, is visible at the top of the spiral, where more advanced decay has attracted woodpeckers who have worked over the older portions of the scar. White pines are good conductors and generally grow taller than other trees in a forest, so are more prone to lightning strikes—information to remember if you ever find yourself in a white pine forest and a thunderstorm is looming.

At this point, take the Footbridge Trail. On the right side at the start of this trail is a hemlock with lots of horizontal lines composed of small holes. These are the sap wells of the yellow-bellied sap-sucker, a woodpecker that taps trees for their sap. In this region,

▲ Rows of sap wells made by generations of yellow-bellied sapsuckers can be seen on this hemlock.

▲ This hemlock was thwarted repeatedly; its trunk was pinned down twice before finding a way to grow upward.

the sapsucker has four favored species of tree: apple, paper birch, basswood, and hemlock. I have always been perplexed by the bird's fidelity to hemlock, but obviously there is something attractive about this tree's sap. The one at the start of the Footbridge Trail has been visited by sapsuckers for many decades, evidenced by the depth and sheer number of sap wells. In this part of their range, ruby-throated hummingbirds also use these sap wells early in the season, when flower nectar is limited.

It might seem that the hummingbirds are parasitizing the sapsuckers, since the sapsuckers do all the work and then have some of their sap consumed by the hummingbirds, but it is more complex than that. Many other birds, insects, and even some mammals feed at the sap wells. When a hummingbird finds a good tree, it vigorously protects it, driving many of the other consumers away—with the exception of the sapsucker, which it lets feed unimpeded. In this way, the hummingbird saves more sap for the sapsucker than it takes, creating a mutually beneficial relationship.

Just before you reach the footbridge, look to your left to see another hemlock—the most contorted tree I have ever encountered. At a young age, the top of this tree was killed, leaving a low limb on its left side to take over as the new trunk. But this limb became pinned down. Eventually it turned to grow up, but was pinned down *again*, growing back to its original starting point. This created a trunk that grew into a long oval before finally being allowed to head upward. It seems to demonstrate that no matter how hard things get, don't give up!

After crossing the bridge, you will come back to the red-blazed trail at the southwestern end of the swamp. Turn left to head back to the cul-de-sac, or continue on to explore another section of this marvelous town forest. There are three other black gum swamps here, although none have trees as old as the main swamp.

MASSACHUSETTS

ELDER'S GROVE

NORTH
ADAMS ② CHARLEMONT

GREENFIELD

② 2

BRYANT HOMESTEAD FOREST

PITTSFIELD CUMMINGTON

91

7

MONUMENT MOUNTAIN

+ GREAT BARRINGTON

+ SHEFFIELD SPRINGFIELD

BARTHOLOMEW'S
COBBLE

AREA OF DETAIL

DUNE
SHACKS
TRAIL

PROVINCETOWN +

Cape Cod
National
Seashore

BEECH FOREST TRAIL

WELLFLEET +

ATLANTIC WHITE
CEDAR SWAMP

6

BARNSTABLE
+

+
FALMOUTH

BEECH FOREST TRAIL

A thriving forest ecosystem rooted in sand

DIFFICULTY
Easy

LOCATION ▸ Cape Cod National Seashore, Provincetown, Massachusetts
FEATURES FOCUS ▸ Grafting, tipped trees

LENGTH
1 mile

The Beech Forest Trail is in the Province Lands portion of the Cape Cod National Seashore. It is a loop trail that you will walk counterclockwise, starting at the right side of the parking area adjacent to Blackwater Pond (the pond is succeeding to a shrubby swamp).

This forest is a remnant of a far more extensive one that covered the Province Lands prior to European settlement. Provincetown was incorporated in 1727 and by 1740, logging and clearing of the forest for pastures had exposed dunes that were previously stabilized for millennia. The much diminished forest is essentially the Province Lands we see today. As you walk through this well-established beech forest, consider that it is growing solely on sand with few nutrients that doesn't hold water very well—yet it is a robust forest ecosystem.

Setting out on the trail, you may notice many black gum trees that are flat topped. These have been sculpted by the consistently strong winds common to this portion of Cape Cod. Along with the black gums, you will find pitch pines and black oaks in the overstory. The understory has inkberry (a strong eco-indicator of sandy soils; often adjacent to wetlands), spotted wintergreen (that also likes sandy substrates), and greenbrier. An interesting thing about spotted wintergreen is that it occurs in all the

▴ Spotted wintergreen, an evergreen understory plant, grows through dead leaves on the forest floor.

▲ Dune erosion has exposed these tree roots.

▲ Wind caused these two sassafras trees to rub through each other's bark, resulting in the trees grafting.

▲ Long ago, foundational sand dunes here were stabilized by the beech forest that grew on top of them.

eastern states, but also occurs in the mountains of Arizona and Mexico as a disjunct population.

Moving down the trail, you will come to stabilized sand dunes. The footpath has caused some erosion at the base of the dunes, evidenced by exposed tree roots to the right of the trail. At the first trail junction, continue straight and enter the section of the forest dominated by American beech. The Beech Forest Trail is composed of two loops—one that goes around Blackwater Pond and another that loops through the beech forest. A little after the trail junction, look to the left for two sassafras trees whose trunks have crossed one another and grafted together. Aboveground grafts like this occur when portions of two trees make contact and wind movement causes them to rub through their bark, over time creating a graft. This is common in beech trees and I have even seen it occur between trees of different species.

Soon you will come to a section of boardwalk that runs through a tight valley flanked on both sides by dunes stabilized long ago by the beech forest. This is quite a unique woodland community—the only well-developed New England beech forest I know of growing on large sand dunes. It offers a very different experience than the Dune Shacks Trail, also in Massachusetts, which explores a section of exposed sand dunes just a little to the east.

Visiting this forest, I noticed a flock of wild turkeys had been foraging in the forest understory. This was evident from all the churned-up leaf litter created as the turkeys scratched the ground looking for nuts, seeds, and insects. Turkeys play an important role in our forests by exposing soil and allowing small-seeded trees to establish. This greatly helps increase the plant diversity in a forest ecosystem.

▲ Stairs climb the stabilized dunes to keep visitors on the trail.

▲ A large sassafras tree grows in the sandy soil here along with an old, hoary red maple behind it.

Soon the trail will take a turn to the left and climb the dune on that side via a stairway. Crest the dune and descend its other side. The trail then runs through another valley. On the right, you will come to a place where people have left the trail to crest the dune on that side, eroding the dune in the process. Please stay on the trail and proceed straight ahead. If enough people keep heading up this unsanctioned gash, in time it will compromise the rare dune ecosystem.

Eventually you will ascend another dune and just as you start to descend its other side, on the right, note a large sassafras tree and behind it an old, hoary red maple. Sassafras is a tree that I think of as an extremist—it seems to only grow in extreme soil conditions. In western New England, I often see it growing on nutrient-rich substrates. The other place I commonly see it is on very sandy soils, as it is here.

In time, take a stairwell down and come back to the portion of the trail that loops around Blackwater Pond. At this junction, go right. The trail runs across the slope of a dune that has good moss coverage on the upper right side.

▲ A section of the trail that goes around Blackwater Pond has extensive mats of moss on its right side.

▲ Large bark plates such as these indicate a pitch pine that is more than 200 years old.

Soon you will leave the beech-forested portion of this exploration and enter a section of forest dominated by pitch pine. On the right side of the trail, there are some old pitch pines with bark plates that are about a foot long and about 3 inches wide. Pitch pines with bark plates this large are at least 200 years old.

On the left side of the trail, looking down toward the pond, are some very contorted black gums. Farther along, you will enter a well-developed pitch pine forest that stabilized the dune on this side of the pond. Walking through this pine forest, look to the right for three pitch pines that all have sharp bends in their trunks close to the ground. The bends are all in the direction of the pond. That's because these pines were tipped over by winds out of the west associated with a thunderstorm. Only thunderstorms in this region produce winds from the west that can blow over trees. After the trees were toppled, either the lowest living branch or activated epicormic buds near the base of their trunks sprouted, generating a new, upward-growing trunk. The downed portion of the original trunk died and decayed away. Epicormic buds on pitch pines can sprout new branches when a portion of the trunk above them has been compromised.

After the bent pitch pines, keep an eye out on the right side of the trail for a root-grafted pitch pine stump. This tree was cut a long time ago, but the stump did not die, even though no epicormic buds were activated to stump sprout. The tree was already root grafted to a neighboring pitch pine, and that has kept the stump alive. This is the only evidence of a root graft I have ever seen in pitch pine, although grafts of this nature are very common in northern white cedar, hemlock, and occasionally occur in white pine.

Next you will come to a trail junction. To the right, you will find a viewing platform overlooking a small pool to the west of Blackwater Pond. Heading straight will return you to the parking lot.

▲ A dune stabilized by a stand of pitch pines.

▲ Three pitch pines were knocked over by the winds of a thunderstorm. Either the lowest living branch or epicormic buds went on to form new trunks.

▲ After being cut, this pitch pine stump survived thanks to a previous root graft with a neighboring tree.

DUNE SHACKS TRAIL

Sand dune climbing, mobile fungi, and cranberries

DIFFICULTY
Difficult

LENGTH
1.5 miles

LOCATION ▸ Provincetown, Massachusetts

FEATURES FOCUS ▸ Glacial impact, math in nature, tipped trees

This out and back hike climbs three large sand dunes and is best done in cool weather or when there is a cloud cover. It traverses very sensitive and fragile ecosystems where increased trail activity could cause serious harm, so I ask you to stay off all vegetation. Keep to the open, exposed sand of the trail to preserve this incredible experience for others who will follow you.

The trail crosses the largest sand dune field in New England. After cresting the three large dunes at its start, you will pass through a series of wonderful ecosystems, ending up at a remote section of beach in the Cape Cod National Seashore. Close to the beach, the trail winds between cabins used by writers and artists through the U.S. National Park Service's seashore residency programs. Please respect the privacy of the people using these cabins by staying on the trail.

The sand that makes up these dunes and much of the Cape was ferried to this region by the Laurentide Ice Sheet—a huge continental glacier that covered what is now eastern Canada and the northeastern United States. It reached its southern extent about 24,000 years ago, creating a terminal moraine that became Long Island, Martha's Vineyard, and Nantucket. The sand is what's left of the glacially eroded, granite bedrock that existed 100 or more miles to the north-northwest of where the Cape lies today. It was deposited as a recessional moraine (debris carried and deposited by a glacier), creating what is now the upper arm of the Cape. Ocean currents took

▲ American dunegrass begins the process of dune stabilization.

▲ On a cloudy day, the second dune beckons from the top of the first dune.

over and carried the sand northward to form the lower arm of the Cape, stretching from Orleans to Provincetown.

The trailhead is on the north side of Route 6. A sign at the start of the trail mentions Eugene O'Neill's use of one of the cabins back in the early 1920s. Just beyond that, you will quickly leave the forest on a ramp of sand and begin the straight-up ascent of the first dune. Unlike the dunes of the Beech Forest Trail, these are very exposed, with little vegetation. The predominant plant that has started the job of stabilizing the dunes is American dunegrass. This is a robust grass that can grow to over 3 feet in height. Its salt tolerance makes it a common plant on dunes adjacent to ocean beaches, and it can handle being buried by windblown sand. This plant clones through extensive rhizomes, making American dunegrass an effective colonizer of exposed sand.

After cresting the first dune, you will descend into a swale, then climb the second and largest dune. Finally, the third dune awaits before you descend into a level area between the dunes and the ocean. Even without much vegetation, these dunes are strikingly beautiful. Take your time crossing them to admire the wonderful surrounding views.

Traveling down the third dune, note clumps of northern bayberry as you approach the stunted stand of pitch pine that dominates the level terrain beyond. Bayberry is common along the coast because of its salt tolerance and its association with root bacteria that fix nitrogen. Its wax-covered fruit is a critical food source for tree swallows

▲ Stunted pitch pine dominates the level terrain beyond the third dune.

during their southern migration; the swallows have adapted to digest the wax, which provides energy for them. Close to the bottom of the dune, the trail runs along a blowout to its left. Blowouts are sandy depressions in dunes where wind has blown away sediments. A close look at the blowout's lip shows that just under the sand is a dark layer of organic material. Much of this is the mycelium of mycorrhizal fungi, which play a critical role in dune ecosystems limited in nutrients and water. Without a mycorrhizal partner, many plants would not be able to colonize these dunes. At the bottom of the blowout, the trail turns left and crosses along its lower margin.

Passing the blowout, you will encounter clumps of sand heather. In autumn these are gray, but come May, the clumps turn green and are covered in dense yellow blossoms. Like bayberry, this shrub has a mutualistic relationship with a bacterium that fixes nitrogen. From mid-summer through fall, keep an eye out for earthstars. These are mycorrhizal fungi that associate with many species of trees, particularly pines and oaks—species that abound between the third dune

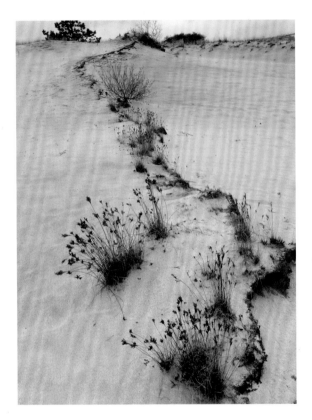

◂ clockwise from left A blowout to the left of the trail hints at the dark organic layer just under the sand. • Sand heather is in its fall gray phase here. • Earthstars such as this one are mycorrhizal fungi that absorb phosphorous and transfer it to their host trees.

and the beach. Earthstars are related to puffballs. They are quite good at absorbing phosphorous and channeling it to their host trees. Like nitrogen, phosphorous is very limited in the sand, thus the need for a partner like the earthstar.

Interestingly, earthstars have a certain amount of mobility. When the outer skin of an earthstar absorbs moisture, it splits into between four and twelve rays that fold down to the ground, exposing the spore sac. The rays can extend down far enough to lift the earthstar up and detach it from its mycelium. This allows the spore sac to tumble across the sand, releasing its spores as it goes.

When you reach the pitch pines, look for one that has cones. Close examination of a cone will show that every seed scale lies at the intersection of a clockwise and counterclockwise spiral. If you count the number of scale spirals that go clockwise around a cone, then the number that go counterclockwise, you will always get two

⏶ Pitch pine cones show the interlocking spirals of their seed scales.

⏶ Bright orange maritime sunburst lichen grows on the bark of a black oak.

consecutive numbers in math's Fibonacci sequence. Whenever interlocking spirals occur in nature, they will always correspond to consecutive numbers in this series.

Scattered among the pitch pines are openings carpeted in moss and reindeer lichen. There are two species of reindeer lichen in this area: the common reindeer lichen that is gray in color and the green reindeer lichen that has a yellow-green color. When these lichens dry, they enter a cryptobiotic state in which they can't perform photosynthesis or any other metabolic function. They are also very brittle in this state and a single footstep will reduce them to dust. However, when they are wet, they feel like a sponge. Regardless of what state they're in when you encounter them, please stay off, although you can gently touch them with your fingers to get a sense of their texture. I have a high regard for moss and reindeer lichen communities. I find them esthetically pleasing. Looking down on them is almost like flying over a forest in late fall; the moss represents coniferous trees and the reindeer lichen reminds me of leafless hardwoods.

Another colorful lichen that can be seen here is the bright orange maritime sunburst lichen. It grows on the bark of some of the black oak trees in with the pitch pines. This lichen needs a certain amount of calcium and can also commonly be seen growing on the mortar of masonry buildings and walls. On the coast of Maine, it is possible to spot where gulls like to perch on the granite shoreline, because those areas of bedrock become coated in sunburst lichen from the calcium in the birds' droppings.

▲ A mat of small cranberry growing on wet sand. The trail runs right through the middle of the cranberries, for easy picking.

One of the attractions of this trail is the many small fens (marshy low lands) along its route. Some of these fens hold water and are dominated by cotton grass, with its fluffy white seed heads, and small cranberry. In autumn many people come out on the Dune Shacks Trail to pick cranberries. In some cases, the cranberries will carpet areas of wet sand that don't hold standing water but are always saturated by the aquifer that lies just beneath the sand.

▲ This weight-bent black oak re-rooted where its upper trunk touched the sand.

Soon you will cross a dune road that services the cabins. On the far side, you will find a black oak that was bent over by weight, most likely from wet snow or ice loading. Where its upper trunk touched the sand, it layered, sending down roots. It now has created a clone of small black oaks growing out of that root system. I have never seen an oak do something like this before, so there are always surprises to be found.

After this bent oak, it is not a long walk to the beach. If you took the Dune Shacks Trail without seeing others, you may end up having this entire section of beach all to yourself.

▲ The end of the Dune Shacks Trail descends to the beach.

ATLANTIC WHITE CEDAR SWAMP

DIFFICULTY
Moderate

LENGTH
1.5 miles

Trees misshapen by nor'easters; a spooky swamp

LOCATION ▸ Wellfleet, Massachusetts

FEATURES FOCUS ▸ Stump sprouts, tipped trees

This sandy trail has one hill climb, on the return from the cedar swamp.

Atlantic white cedar used to be more common than it is today. This is the result of so many New England white cedar swamps being logged for the tree's rot-resistant wood. Like the Manchester Cedar Swamp in New Hampshire, this one also has old trees. However, the Atlantic White Cedar Swamp is far larger than the one in Manchester and may be the best example in New England of this rare ecosystem.

The path to the swamp starts as a level trail through a stunted forest of pitch pine and bear oak. Bear oak is an eco-indicator of dry, nutrient-poor soils and is found both in sandy substrates, as it is here, as well as rock outcrops. The stunting of this forest is due to severe wind exposure. Lying right at the top of the fore dune of the Marconi Wireless Station Site, this forest takes the brunt of both hurricane and nor'easter winds—the latter often associated with wet snow that causes a lot of canopy breakage. When you come to the fork in the trail, go left.

Along with the pitch pine and bear oak are bayberry and mats of bearberry—a classic Cape Cod community. Many of the bear oaks are encrusted with species of lichen, thanks to their close presence to the ocean and the fog it generates. Continuing on the trail and starting to descend, you will notice the pitch pine trees grow taller, creating a closed-crown forest that reduces the presence of the bear oak. The severe winds closer to the fore dune reduce the number of pitch pines, allowing more bear oak. (Even though the wind contorts the oaks, it is benefiting them by reducing competition from the pines.)

▲ The path to the cedar swamp starts in a stunted stand of pitch pine and bear oak.

▲ Contortions in these pitch pine and bear oak trunks are the result of repeated breakages in their canopies, mostly caused by nor'easters.

As the canopy of the pitch pines continues to rise, more light reaches the understory, ushering in a new species—broom crowberry. This is a rather uncommon plant in New England, usually restricted to the coastal fringe on sandy substrates, or in Maine on granite bedrock. It usually associates with pitch pine. It is one of the region's earliest bloomers, putting forth minute red flowers in late March through early April. When you see this plant, you may mistake it for a moss because its leaves are tiny, smaller than a grain of rice. However, examine it more closely and you will see it has a woody stem. It may not look like much to a casual observer, but its presence indicates that you have entered a rare ecological community of New England.

Continuing on, look for an old pitch pine on the left that has a bent trunk near the ground. This tree was tipping when it was young, and like the bent pitch pines on the Beech Forest Trail, it sprouted a new trunk that grew upward, while the original trunk died and decayed away. However, shortly after the new trunk took off, it was broken and a side branch took over, creating an additional elbow.

Closer to the swamp, you will descend into a small valley and the forest will shift from pitch pine to red oak, with highbush blueberry in the understory. Cross a woods road and you will come to a coppiced white oak on the left that has four trunks. This tree was cut when it was about 18 inches in diameter, well over a century ago—possibly even two centuries. It then stump sprouted new trunks. This

▲ The floor of this pitch pine forest is carpeted in the uncommon broom crowberry.

tree is very close to the boardwalk loop that will take you through the swamp. When you reach the loop, go left.

As you enter the Atlantic White Cedar Swamp, you will be going into an ecosystem with few plant species. The swamp is dominated by a dense stand of cedars with scattered red maples. Winterberry holly is found here and there in the understory and sphagnum mosses cover the swamp's hummocks. With adequate light, winterberry holly can produce dense clusters of bright red berries. During a recent fall, this holly produced a bumper crop of berries throughout New England. Here, in the dense shade of the cedar, few berries are likely to be found.

Although this swamp hosts few plant species, it is still a treat to walk through. The cedars come in all shapes that create kind of an eerie effect. Maybe an idea for a hike on Halloween? Many of these cedars have obvious spirals in their trunks. Most tree trunks spiral to the right as one looks up the tree. In my experience, Atlantic white cedars may be the exception, because the majority I have encountered twist to the left, as is readily apparent in this swamp. Although the trees here are not huge, they are old—the larger, more tightly spiraled individuals most likely exceed 200 years of age.

When you reach the end of the boardwalk, you will leave the swamp and reenter a pitch pine–bear oak woodland. Cross the woods road again and begin your ascent back to the stunted forest that first greeted you on this exploration.

▲ clockwise from above An old pitch pine that was bent when it was young and then had a breakage event has multiple elbows near its base. • A coppiced white oak with four trunks that stump sprouted when the original tree was cut, between 100 and 200 years ago. • Trunk spirals on most Atlantic white cedars I've seen turn to the left—the opposite direction of most other tree species.

ELDERS GROVE

Favorable conditions give rise to remarkably tall trees

DIFFICULTY
Moderate

LENGTH
1 mile

LOCATION ▸ Charlemont, Massachusetts

FEATURES FOCUS ▸ Basal fire scars, glacial impact, stump sprouts

The Elders Grove Trail in Mohawk Trail State Forest is a round-trip hike with some sections of irregular footing and one uphill section that is a few hundred feet long.

This exploration is unique for its stand of very tall white pines—many of which exceed 170 feet. Even more striking is that these are not old-growth pines, but rather middle-aged trees that are still growing vigorously. If this stand can continue free of disturbance, by the middle of this century there should be trees approaching 200 feet in height. Here in New England, where 100 feet is thought of as tall, that is a remarkable accomplishment!

The trail starts at the west end of the bridge crossing the Deerfield River just below Zoar Gap—a favorite rafting site in western Massachusetts. It runs adjacent to the river all the way to Elders Grove. Parking can be found on the eastern end of the bridge, across Zoar Road. As you walk across the bridge to access the trail, look both north and south. To the south of the bridge is the Todd-Clark ridgeline and to the north Negus Mountain. The forests on each of these opposing slopes are very dissimilar due to different substrates and topographic settings.

When you turn to Negus Mountain, you will be looking at its steep south-facing slope. Because of all the sunlight it receives, that side of Negus is a hot, dry site. The bedrock of the mountain also produces nutrient-poor soils. As a result, this south slope of Negus supports lots of red oaks and an understory of mountain laurel—species that can tolerate warm, dry, acidic sites. A closer look at the forest on this south-facing slope will show that there is age discontinuity, with scattered large red oaks and then many much smaller

▴ View of the Deerfield River from the bridge.

birches, but no trees of intermediate size. This is akin to the age discontinuity found on Wantastiquet Mountain in New Hampshire—in both cases, the discontinuity is the result of wildfire. The largest trees can survive the heat of a blaze when it burns through. Trees with smaller trunks are killed outright. But if the heat-killed trunks are hardwoods, they will stump sprout, creating multi-trunked trees. The ensuing forest then lacks trees of intermediate size.

The rail line that goes through the Hoosac Tunnel runs right at the base of Negus Mountain and has sparked fires over the years that race up the mountain's south slope. At the end of your exploration of Elders Grove, it is worth a short bushwhack from your car to the base of Negus, where you will see ample evidence of past fires, particularly basal fire scars on the larger trees, plus lots of coppiced trees.

In contrast, the Todd-Clark ridgeline has a steep north-facing slope and is underlain by calcium-enriched bedrock, creating a cool, moist, rich site that supports lots of trees that need calcium, such as white ash, green ash, and bitternut hickory. This north-facing slope is also composed of talus—large blocks of rock that broke off a cliff to form an apron of jumbled boulders at its base. Most of this talus was formed shortly after the Laurentide Ice Sheet departed from this region more than 15,000 years ago, when the Todd-Clark cliff was exposed to frequent freeze-thaw cycles that levered rock from its cliff face. Walking on talus is challenging and potentially dangerous; be sure to use care.

Trees on this north slope grow very tall. The calcium-enriched talus creates fertile soils and the large blocks of rock allow trees to firmly anchor themselves on the site as their roots grow around the large boulders. The orientation of the slope protects the trees from wind disturbance and forces them to grow up, because light on a north slope is more limited. The result is that these trees grow quickly and really stretch out.

It is generally thought that trees slow their rates of growth at about 80 years and have been considered to be overmature when they surpass that age. But recent tree measuring clearly shows that is not the case. Using the big pines in the Elders Grove, it's been found that even trees around 175 years old are still increasing their growth rates, making older trees impressive carbon sinks.

About 20 years ago, I was invited to explore this slope and help laser measure some of its trees. We were taken aback at the close of that day, because on the north slope of the Todd-Clark ridgeline, we recorded the tallest heights ever measured in northeastern trees for specimens of nine species, including the tallest white ash, sugar maple, and beech. All exceeded 130 feet!

The trail enters the woods and soon turns to the left to follow the Deerfield River. After you cross the first footbridge, look to your left for a large green ash. Green and white ash have bark that I think resembles the pattern on the rind of a cantaloupe. However, they can be differentiated because the bark of green ash is squishy and can be compressed by pushing on it, like cork. The bark of white ash is solid and can't be compressed. Green ash is usually found near rivers and streams as it is here, because it likes moist, rich soils. Be sure to push the bark of this green ash to confirm its squishiness.

After the second footbridge, on the left you will find a white ash and you can test its bark's firmness. Finally, just after the third bridge, on the right side of the trail are two trees whose bark looks

▴ White ash bark resembles the pattern on the rind of a cantaloupe.

▴ An attempted girdle by a beaver was not successful in killing this hemlock.

similar. The one to the right is a bitternut hickory and the one to the left is another white ash. I think of bitternut hickory as having a bark pattern very similar to ash, but it appears to have been ironed to make it look smoother. Bitternut hickory bark fissures are also very shallow compared to those of ash. Both of these trees like the rich, moist soils they find at this site. Forests dominated by white ash and bitternut hickory occur on our region's richest sites, and are places to visit in late April and early May when woodland vernal wildflowers are in bloom. Even after blooming is finished, these sites can be iden-tified by robust stands of maidenhair fern and blue cohosh.

As you continue down the trail, look to the left for hemlocks girdled (cambial tissue beneath bark is destroyed in a ring around the trunk) by beavers, as was discussed in the chapter on Pisgah State Park in New Hampshire. The strong flow of the Deerfield River means that beavers can't dam it. Instead, they make bank lodges by burrowing into a riverbank below the surface of the water and then excavating upward to make a nice, dry, underground chamber.

Along the way you will come to many clumps of hobblebush—a viburnum with opposite, rounded leaves. This is a shrub that does quite well in shady, cool sites such as this one. In the fall, it has beautiful leaf coloration. In one leaf it is possible to have green, yellow, orange, red, purple, and blue hues.

In time, the trail will gently head down and be directly adjacent to the river before it starts its uphill climb to the Elders Grove. About three-quarters of the way up the climb, look across the slope to the right of the trail. Many of the white ash you see will be over 130 feet in height, and don't start branching until about 80 feet. Since everything on this slope is tall, it is hard to gauge height. One way is to find an ash with a large basal scar facing the trail. That scar is about 5 feet high, so using it as a reference will help you sense that the tree is indeed tall.

As the trail levels out, you will enter the Elders Grove. It has a couple dozen white pines that range between 150 and 180 feet tall and are up to 4 feet or more in diameter. Each tall pine here has been named after a Native American elder, which is the reason the site is called the Elders Grove. All of these trees have a height tag. They were measured before 2010 and have put on a foot or more per year since then, so you can add some feet to the reading on each tree's tag. Looking downhill from the trail, you may see a number of trees with uphill basal scars, indicating a former fire on this site.

Entering the Elders Grove, where trees have been named after Native American elders. ▸

▲ An uphill basal fire scar on one of the white pines.

▲ Two pines in the Elders Grove with more than 4-foot diameters.

▲ Looking up the trunk of a pine over 170 feet tall.

There is another puzzling feature at this site: numerous small piles of stones. If the stone piles occurred right along the path, we could surmise they were rocks cleared from the trail. That is not the case, though, because they can be found throughout the site. Stone piles also indicate a former crop field. That is also not the case here, because the ground is covered in pillows and cradles and was never plowed. Since the pines are closing in on 200 years, it means this site was never opened for any kind of agriculture and has always been forest. Why would one or more people be out in these woods collecting and making small stone piles? I am pretty good at inferring what has happened in woodlands, but have absolutely no explanation. This is truly one of the few times I have been stumped trying to interpret a forest's history.

The most impressive feature of this stand is its pines. They top out way above the hardwood trees that share the site, as they soar into the canopy. There is no other stand of pine that holds this many tall trees anywhere in the Northeast, making it a truly remarkable experience. For someone used to redwoods or large Douglas firs, standing at the base of one of these pines and looking up the length of its trunk might not be such a big deal. However, compared to our other regional trees, such a view is awe inspiring.

BRYANT HOMESTEAD FOREST

Old-growth pockets on William Cullen Bryant's summer property

DIFFICULTY
Moderate

LENGTH
1 mile

LOCATION ▸ Cummington, Massachusetts

FEATURES FOCUS ▸ Old growth, pillows and cradles, stone walls and early agriculture, white pine weevil

This loop trail has generally good footing and a gentle 200-foot climb at the end of the walk.

William Cullen Bryant—one of America's great poets—was the editor and publisher of the *New York Evening Post* for 50 years. This property was his summer home and is now owned by The Trustees of Reservations. It is also a designated National Historical Landmark. The forest you are going to explore has pockets of old growth and influenced a number of Bryant's poems.

An interesting side note is that The Trustees of Reservations was the brainchild of Charles Elliot and the very first land trust, not only in this country, but in the world. Charles was the son of Harvard president Charles W. Elliot who, during summers, would sail his family up to Mount Desert Island in Maine. In 1880, his son Charles Elliot sailed a group of Harvard undergraduates—of which he was one—up to Mount Desert Island to spend the summer camping and exploring the natural history of what was to become Acadia National Park. During that summer, young Elliot came up with the radical idea that a group of private citizens should buy much of the land on Mount Desert Island and protect it to create a natural park that could be enjoyed by the general public. With that seed planted, Elliot went on to become a landscape architect. In 1890 he re-hatched his idea to protect land, this time in the Boston environs. In 1891 The Trustees of Public Reservations was established to do just that. What makes this story so interesting is that all the land trusts that exist in the world today were inspired by a 21-year-old student.

The Rivulet Trail starts in a forest of weevil-hit white pines that also has smooth and even ground. The pines were about 60 years old when I visited, which means that what was previously open land was abandoned around 1960, and that the site was plowed at one time, which removed its pillows and cradles. Just after post 2, you will step into a forest of older weevil-hit pines that was abandoned around the end of World War II. The ground becomes covered in pillows and cradles. Because there is no bottom-plow terrace (described in the chapter on Bomoseen State Park in Vermont) between the smooth, even ground and the pillows and cradles, it means that you went from an abandoned hayfield into a pasture that was also abandoned a decade or so earlier. (A bottom-plow terrace is a level area at the base of a sloping crop field. There is no evidence of that feature here.)

As you continue down the trail, look to the left for a white pine hit by a lightning strike around 2010. We can date the strike by counting the number of annual growth lines on the bark of the callus that is slowly growing over the wound. Since the strike runs almost straight up the tree with little spiraling, it means this pine was fast in its vertical growth. Slow-growing trees develop tight trunk spirals.

The forest changes from white pine to a mix of hardwoods and hemlock, with some trees approaching 200 years of age. This indicates that you have now left the abandoned pasture and entered an area that has always been forest. The remainder of your walk will be in this continuously forested parcel that has pockets of old growth.

When the Rivulet Trail forks, go left and notice the large pillows and cradles that are often typical of always-forested areas. Also keep an eye out for an ancient green ash on the left side of the trail. I don't know exactly how old this tree might

▲ A lightning scar that travels fairly straight up a white pine shows that the trunk grew quickly, with little of the usual spiraling that accompanies slow growth.

be, however, it is without a doubt the largest and oldest green ash I have ever encountered.

Continuing on, sections of the trail are carpeted in roundleaf yellow violet. It is also known as early yellow violet, because it is often the first violet to flower in mid-April. This plant can be identified when not in flower by its roundish leaves that hug the ground. Most other violets have heart-shaped leaves that stand up higher. Also noticeable on this trail is the large number of downed trees. These create what ecologists call coarse woody debris (CWD). It may not look like much, but it is critical for the well-being of a forest ecosystem—many species of decomposers rely on it. Studies in Britain have shown that over 20,000 species can inhabit one large snag. As we have moved toward whole-tree harvesting in logging operations over the past few decades, coarse woody debris has declined in our forests. This reduces the biotic diversity in our forests, making them less resilient. Today the Black Forest in Germany is being seriously impacted by air pollution. Areas that have been picked clean of their CWD to keep them looking tidy are suffering the most, because they are not as resilient as parts of the forest that have retained their CWD.

A number of black birch seedlings grow in the moss covering a white pine nurse log. ▸

Downed trunks of white pines have another function. They serve as nurse logs for small-seeded, shade-tolerant trees like black birch, yellow birch, and hemlock. After about 20 years, a downed pine trunk will have shed its bark. By 30 years, it will support a nice bed of moss that is the perfect germination site for small seeds. Since the log decays slowly from the outside, it gives trees plenty of time to snake their roots down the log and into the ground. Eventually, when the log has completely decayed, it will leave a row of stilted-root trees with aboveground roots linking them together.

When you reach the junction with the Pine Loop Trail, take a left. You will soon enter a well-developed forest of tall white pines. These trees are not old growth, but still quite impressive. Keep an eye out for a white quartz boulder on the left side of the trail. Look closely at this boulder and you can see pieces have been broken off. In the town of Westminster, Vermont, there are intrusions of white quartz in the bedrock that have seams of silver in them. That

▲ A stand of tall pines on the Pine Loop Trail; note the obvious pillows on the forest floor.

▲ This white quartz boulder may have been broken apart to extract silver in its seams.

▲ Two white pines. The one on the left can be identified as an old-growth tree by its coarse bark plates.

Vermont bedrock has been quarried for silver and the same may be the case with this boulder.

Eventually the trail will take a turn to the right and you will enter a section of forest with very large pillows and cradles—many with pines growing on them. These pits and mounds were created by western winds generated during a thunderstorm. We know this because only thunderstorms produce tree-toppling winds out of the west. It would take at least 50 years for the roots of a downed tree to decay to form pillows of this size. Because the pines growing on them are close to 200 years old, it means this thunderstorm occurred around the time of the Revolutionary War. As you emerge from this old blowdown, you will enter a section of forest that has old-growth white pine trees. This can be inferred by the size of the trees' bark plates.

At the junction with the Rivulet Trail, head left and you will enter an old-growth stand of mixed hemlock and hardwoods. Cross a bridge, and on the right side of the trail is an old-growth hemlock that has chartreuse-green lichen growing on its bark. I have never seen this lichen growing on the bark of a hemlock unless the tree exceeds 275 years of age. With such a large amount of this lichen, it's highly likely this hemlock is more than 350 years old.

The forest becomes younger after this old hemlock. If you are here in summer, look for Indian pipe—a white, non-photosynthetic flowering plant—in the understory. Indian pipe is a member of the heath family, and like all heaths, it has to associate with

▲ The lichen on this old-growth hemlock reveals it is likely more than three and a half centuries old.

▲ White, non-photosynthetic Indian pipe needs no light, so it can grow in heavy shade.

mycorrhizal fungi. This is where the plant gets its energy, because it can't photosynthesize. Since it is not dependent on light, it often grows in deep shade.

Keep an eye out for post 8. At this point on the right side of the trail is a huge, old-growth black cherry. Once again, like the green ash encountered earlier, this is the largest and oldest specimen of black cherry that I have ever encountered, making the Bryant Homestead Forest quite special. At the last trail junction, go left to head back to the parking area.

MONUMENT MOUNTAIN

Ferns growing on stone and a cave
that influenced Moby-Dick

DIFFICULTY
Difficult

LENGTH
2.5 miles

LOCATION ▸ Great Barrington, Massachusetts

FEATURES FOCUS ▸ Chestnut blight, pillows and cradles, stone walls and early agriculture, tree secrets: black birch, white pine weevil

The Trustees of Reservations have a number of exceptional properties, and this is one of them. It's a loop trail that gains 700 feet vertically. Access is free if you are a member of The Trustees, otherwise there is a $5 fee.

Start on the yellow-blazed Hickey Trail to the right of the parking area. Entering the forest, you will find the ground smooth and even, from plowing for a former hayfield or crop field. It is a good growing site, supporting tall white and red pines as well as black cherry and sassafras.

The trail ascends gently at first and in time will come to a large doubled-trunked white oak on the left side of the trail. Each trunk of this tree is about 20 inches in diameter; the original trunk was cut when it was about 30 inches in diameter. The acorn of this tree germinated about the time of the Revolutionary War, which means the trail has entered an area that has always been a forest. Looking around, you will see lots of red oak with an understory of witch hazel, but no pines.

I can report that in November, after the oaks have dropped their leaves, walking the steep trail becomes difficult due to the slippery nature of the downed leaves; you may want to make this

▴ A large, old, double-trunked white oak. The original single-trunked tree started growing around the time of the Revolutionary War.

◂ Rock polypody fern covers the tops of quartzite talus boulders.

trip earlier in the year. Eventually, it will climb steeply to the base of a talus slope composed of quartzite boulders that have cleaved off the cliff on the eastern side of this mountain. The tops of the boulders are all covered by the lush growth of rock polypody—a small-statured fern that pretty much only grows on the tops of boulders with very thin soils. I'm always struck by this robust-looking plant, with its shiny, dark green leaves, residing on one of the driest of growing sites. However, one advantage of this xeric site is that nothing else can tolerate the dryness—removing all competition for the polypody. The cavities in the talus slope make great den sites for porcupine. Many of the hemlocks near the talus slope have somewhat deformed canopies from the repeated browsing of this herbivore.

The trail then turns away from the talus slope and continues to climb. On the right, look for an American chestnut with a dead snag and stump sprouts. When I did this trail, the trunk of the chestnut had orange spores emerging through its bark from the chestnut blight fungus. The leaves of the chestnut should be visible at all times since they are marcescent, which means they stay attached to branches and do not drop in autumn after they die. I think chestnut leaves are quite elegant with their long, tapering, toothed margins.

Soon the trail will turn left and start to level out. Along this section are a number of old-growth white pines, and a fine example

▲ Orange spores from the chestnut blight fungus can be seen on this chestnut tree.

▲ Old-growth white pine is distinguished by its coarse bark plates.

▲ The leaves of the American chestnut stay attached and do not fall when they die in autumn.

▲ The cave that helped inspire Herman Melville in writing *Moby-Dick*.

with large bark plates is visible here on the left. These trees are probably close to 300 years old. Eventually the trail will run along the lip of a steep-walled ravine to its right. It will then cross the stream that created the ravine and run into some tulip trees, whose bark looks like white ash but lacks the stout, oppositely arranged twigs of the ash. On the right of the trail, look for a hemlock growing on a nurse stump. This is an unusual example, because most nurse stumps are white pine. In this case the stump is a red oak, which can

▲ A large burl at the base of a red maple, just before the stairway to the ridgetop.

▲ Stairs that climb to the ridgetop, here covered by autumn leaves.

be discerned by the reddish brown color of the decaying wood. On the left is a small cave with a waterfall, from the stream you crossed, plunging over it.

This cave has historic significance. On August 5, 1850, publisher David Dudley Field invited Oliver Wendell Holmes, Nathaniel Hawthorn, and Herman Melville to hike Monument Mountain with him. At this point in the hike, a thunderstorm broke out and the four men sought refuge in the cave. While sheltering in the cave, their discussion inspired the direction of Melville's masterwork, *Moby-Dick*.

Continuing on, you will come to a stairway that leads to the ridgetop. Before you get to the stairs, on your right, you'll see a red maple with an example of a large burl at the base of its trunk.

On the ridgetop, the forest becomes much younger and is composed of red oak. The trail turns to the left, crosses a stream, then starts to climb again and crosses over some quartzite talus. Mountain laurel becomes prominent. Finally, you will reach the end of the Hickey Trail at Inscription Rock, which commemorates the preservation of Monument Mountain in 1899 by The Trustees of Reservations. From here, you can continue up to the top of the mountain for the views on the Squaw Peak Trail. A word of caution: part of the Squaw Peak Trail is a knife-edged ridge with steep drops on either side, plus the quartzite is slippery and the footing very irregular. Only experienced, sure-footed hikers should attempt this trail.

At Inscription Rock, take Indian Mountain Trail, which starts on the right at the end of Hickey Trail. As you head down, this trail becomes entrenched almost 5 feet below the surrounding oak forest. The only explanation for this is that it must have been a carriage road that has significantly eroded over time. After you pass through this lower section, the forest changes to an older one dominated by white pine and hemlock. The trail parallels a talus slope to its left and eventually becomes entrenched once again.

Just after the Squaw Peak Trail joins the Indian Mountain Trail, look to the left for a black birch with many burls on its trunk. Because this birch has shed almost all of its rectangular bark plates and now has smooth bark without lenticels, it is about 150 years old.

The forest will change again to a stand of weevil-hit white pines that colonized an abandoned pasture around 1960. This interpretation is based on the presence of pillows and cradles on the site, and the dominance of weevil-hit pines. Next you will come to a wall of quartzite rocks with a lot of small stones in it. This wall separated the pasture from a crop field. The numerous small stones in the wall and the even ground on the far side of the wall tell that story.

The trail then turns to the left and heads toward Route 7. Make another turn to the left to walk parallel to the road. On the left side of the trail, notice the rounded quartzite glacial boulders, which are in contrast to the talus boulders you have previously seen.

Continuing, you will come to a very old, coppiced chestnut oak with three large trunks. This tree was most likely cut in the early 1800s, then three trunks stump sprouted from the original. The size of the original trunk can be estimated by drawing a circle at ground level through the centers of their existing trunks. This tree's trunk was about 30 inches in diameter when it was logged, so it was over a century old when it was cut—and started growing around 1700 or earlier. After this oak, it is a short walk back to the parking area.

▲ A portion of the trail was likely an old carriage road that today is entrenched below the surrounding forest.

▲ An old, triple-trunked chestnut oak whose original acorn probably sprouted around 1700.

BARTHOLOMEW'S COBBLE

Quartzite, marble, and more than 800 plant species

DIFFICULTY
Moderate

LENGTH
2 miles

LOCATION ▸ Sheffield, Massachusetts

FEATURES FOCUS ▸ Tipped trees, stone walls and early agriculture, white pine weevil

This is a gentle trail with good footing. Like Monument Mountain, there is a $5 fee if you are not a member of The Trustees of Reservations.

Bartholomew's Cobble is the most botanically diverse site of all the locations covered in this book. There are two reasons for this wide-reaching diversity. The first is that the cobble—which means "rocky knoll" here—actually has two such knolls, or ledge outcrops—one composed of quartzite and the other of marble. These outcrops provide a high number of microenvironments for plants. The second explanation is the mix of upland and floodplain soils here. Together, these features allow the cobble to support more than 800 species of plants. Possibly the cobble's biggest asset is that it hosts the greatest diversity of fern species in all of North America! Because of its ample plant diversity, the cobble is a National Natural Landmark, through the U.S. National Parks Service.

This exploration starts on the Ledges Trail to the left of the Visitors Center. On the right side, at the start of the trail, is an outcropping of marble covered in moss. The marble also supports both rock polypody and maidenhair spleenwort ferns. The latter is widely distributed across the globe and has numerous subspecies—each of which is specialized to grow on a different kind of rock. In this case, the subspecies grows on marble. Maidenhair spleenwort may be my

▲ A classic moss-covered marble outcrop at the cobble.

▲ A subspecies of maidenhair spleenwort grows on exposed marble.

favorite fern. Although small in stature, with leaves just a few inches long, it is tough and can grow all by itself on naked rock.

The Ledges Trail runs along the base of marble outcrops that generate nutrient-enriched soils. Calciferous plants that do well here include blue cohosh, maidenhair fern, herb Robert, red columbine, and round-lobed hepatica. As the trail approaches the Housatonic River, keep an eye to the left for a weight-bent black birch. This birch was most likely bent over at a young age by wet snow or ice loading. The lowest branch then took over as the new trunk, while the original trunk died and rotted away. On the right side of the trail, across from the birch, is a vertical moss-covered face of marble that has what looks like blades of sedge hanging down from the moss. This is actually walking fern, an uncommon fern restricted to marble and limestone. It gets its name from the fact that when the tip of a blade touches the moss out of which it grows, it re-roots at that point and sprouts more leaves, similar to layering in trees. After this outcrop, you will descend some stairs and be adjacent to the river.

As the trail continues, look to the right to see a robust poison ivy vine growing up a white ash tree. Poison ivy vines are easy to identify by their numerous reddish, aerial rootlets that attach the vines to a tree. Like the sassafras I mentioned in the chapter on the Beech Forest Trail, poison ivy is an extremist to me—a plant that grows in extreme soils. As with sassafras, poison ivy thrives in rich, moist soils as well as very poor, dry soils such as sand. The only

▲ This black birch was bent by wet snow or ice loading when it was young.

▲ The Housatonic River, part of the Bartholomew's Cobble ecosystem.

place it is uncommon is in moderate soils. There is a lot of poison ivy at the cobble thanks to its rich, moist soils. A photo of poison ivy growing on a tree trunk appears in the chapter on Oakland Forest in Rhode Island.

A little farther along, on the left, is Corbin's Neck, a peninsula created by an oxbow in the Housatonic River. Eventually a flood will breach the base of the neck and the river will flow parallel and close to the trail. The current oxbow will be cut off from the river, forming an oxbow lake. Currently, Corbin's Neck is used as a dairy pasture. Examining the trees that grow between the pasture and the trail, you will find a great many species, including hackberry, sugar maple, bitternut hickory, beech, red oak, basswood, shagbark hickory, American elm, musclewood, and hop hornbeam. Hackberry is identified by its vertical, warty ridges, which grow here and there on its trunk. Many of these species like enriched soils and the American elm and hackberry are alluvial floodplain specialists. This little cluster of trees is a good example of the cobble's wonderful plant diversity.

When you reach the junction with Cedar Hill Trail, go left and stay on Ledges Trail. The trail will go up a set of stairs and then pass between two old white pines. At this point, look to the right to find some round-lobed hepatica. When you come to sign post 12, if you are here in summer, you will get a special treat.

The marble ledge is overhung and at its base is exposed, fine sand. If you look at the sand close to the bedrock, you should see some conical depressions in it. These are the pit traps of ant lion larvae. If an ant, or other insect, wanders into one of these traps, the larva buried at the base of the pit tosses up sand to knock the insect to the bottom of the pit—where two sharp mandibles are waiting to grab it and pull it under the sand to be eaten. There is a scene in one of the *Star Wars* movies where Jabba the Hutt intends to kill Luke Skywalker by having him thrown into a pit of sand. Undoubtedly, this scene was inspired by real-life ant lions. These insects are pretty uncommon. In fact, this is just one of three sites where I have seen them.

▲ The overhanging marble ledge on the right has ant lion pit traps at its base.

Shortly after the ant lion pits, turn left onto Bailey Trail. Then cross a bridge that goes over an ephemeral stream and enter a stand of weevil-hit white pines on a site that was abandoned around 1950. Since the ground lacks pillows and cradles, it was plowed in the past to create either a hay-

▲ A beaver attempted to girdle this hemlock in 2008.

field or a crop field. Keep an eye to the right side of the trail for a huge moss-covered grape vine. The grape, white ash, and bitternut hickory tell us these are nutrient-rich, moist soils—a good place to grow crops. After crossing the second bridge, you will transition into floodplain soils, with a lot of eastern cottonwood—another specialist to these alluvial sites. After the third bridge, look to the right for a hemlock that a beaver attempted to girdle (to destroy the cambium under the bark in a ring around the trunk). When I was here in 2019, I counted eleven growth lines on the bark of the callus growing on the right side of the wound, so the beaver did this in 2008.

Cross the fourth bridge and on the right you'll find a large American elm with buttresses at the base of its trunk covered in moss. Eventually, you will enter a stand of weevil-hit pine from land abandoned in the late 1800s on the right of the trail. To the left of the trail is an alluvial, floodplain forest dominated by silver maple. In older floodplain stands, silver maple will always dominate. Soon you will reach the junction with Spero Trail, and the largest eastern cottonwood I have ever seen, with a trunk diameter of about 7 feet. This tree was hit by lightning and is also hollowed out.

Turn left onto Spero Trail to walk it clockwise. The floodplain forest you enter will be dominated by silver maple, which commonly have trunks that fork close to the forest floor. Along with the silver maple are white ash, bitternut hickory, American elm, and hackberry. The understory of this forest has a lot of ostrich fern, which has a brown fertile frond shaped like a feather, and whose fronds grow 3 to 4 feet in height. This is the fern that produces edible fiddleheads that are picked in April. Just before you leave this floodplain forest, there is a very large, triple-trunked silver maple on the left. Here you can turn around and head back, or continue on to complete Spero Trail.

If you decide to continue, you will enter a former hayfield that was abandoned around 2014 and planted with alluvial floodplain species, including two new species that specialize to such sites: American sycamore and box elder.

▲ Looking up the largest cottonwood I have ever encountered.

The trail eventually runs right next to the river in a second field. Here, between the trail and the river, is a natural levee—a raised lip next to the river—that was created by repeated flooding. As soon as floodwaters crest a riverbank, their velocity slows, allowing sand and silts they are carrying to be deposited, forming the levee. Eventually you will leave the fields and enter an upland forest dominated by red oak and black cherry. The forest will shift to hemlock, with scattered, old, coppiced red oaks and white pines that signify this area has always been a forest. When you come to your first bridge crossing on Spero Trail, there is a well-developed oxbow lake to the right.

▲ With my wife as reference, I estimate the base of this cottonwood at around 7 feet in diameter.

Go straight when you come to the junction with Bailey Trail. When you get back to Ledges Trail, go left. Soon after, there is a fork, with the trail going right and a farm road going left—go right along the edge of the cobble. Looking up, you will see some old eastern red cedars growing on the bedrock. On outcrops like this, with extreme growing conditions to restrict competition, red cedars can grow older than 300 years. These trees are not yet that old, but in time may reach three centuries.

RHODE ISLAND

TILLINGHAST
POND

+
WEST
GREENWICH

95

AREA OF DETAIL

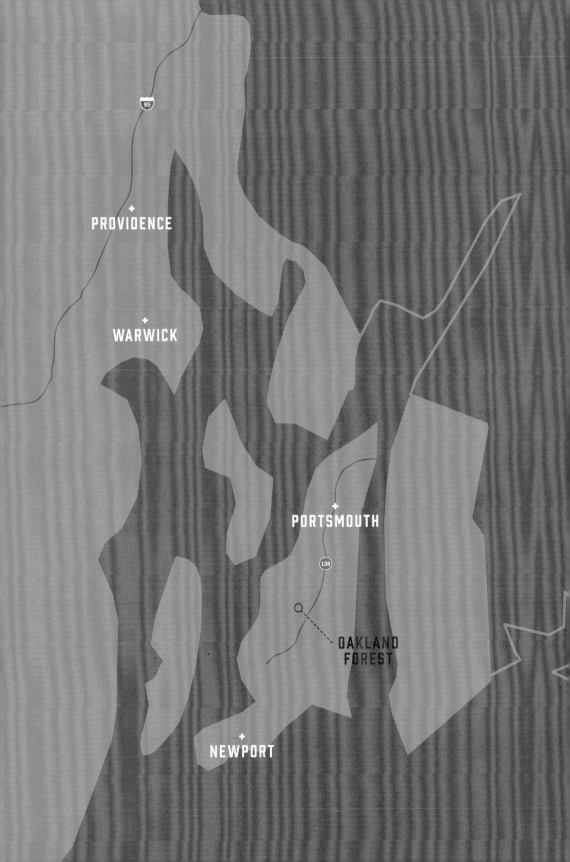

OAKLAND FOREST

Unusual old-growth beech stand
left unscarred by disease

DIFFICULTY
Easy

LOCATION ▸ Portsmouth, Rhode Island
FEATURES FOCUS ▸ Beech bark scale, grafting, old growth, tipped trees, tree secrets: black gum

LENGTH
.75 miles

A wildflower meadow accompanies the start of the trail; visit in October to see the goldenrod in bloom.

Parking at this trailhead is quite limited, so be forewarned. The trail is short and level. Oakland Forest and Meadow Trail will take you into an old-growth stand dominated by beech, with scattered old-growth white oaks and black gums. Particularly fortunate about this forest is that the beech are healthy and have no sign of beech bark scale disease that has infiltrated other regional stands. Thanks to the old-growth and healthy status of these beech trees, this is truly a unique ecosystem for New England. Perhaps surprisingly, the Oakland Forest is surrounded by suburban housing developments in the town of Portsmouth. Luckily, this unusual property is protected by the Aquidneck Land Trust.

The trail begins by skirting a wildflower field that must be gorgeous in October, because it is loaded with goldenrod. Eventually, the trail enters the woods. The Oakland Forest has two sections, which are divided by a planted belt of rhododendrons that runs through the center of the woodland. The first half of the forest is a natural, old-growth stand composed of beech, white oak, black gum, red maple, and red oak. Right at the start, you will encounter old black gums with deformed canopies from multiple breakage events over the years. Farther north in New England, black gum is pretty much restricted to swamps. In the Oakland Forest it is well represented, growing in a dry, upland setting.

▲ Many of the black gums here have crooked branches from being repeatedly broken.

▲ A mass of sprouts around this old black gum leads me to believe there may be a tumorous growth in its root system.

The trail runs along the edge of the forest and you will come to an aged yellow birch on the left, before the trail takes a turn to the right and heads deeper into the woods. Just after the trail takes this turn, look to the right for an old black gum that has a dense stand of young root sprouts around it. This is the only example I have ever seen of a black gum doing this, so I am guessing it is caused by some form of tumorous growth in its surficial root system.

The trail will lead to a loop that runs through the forest. Just before you reach the junction with the loop trail, there is an unusual beech to the left. This tree is composed of two trunks that grew close to each other and eventually grafted at their base. The low, horizontal trunk on the left was bent over by weight (perhaps snow or ice) and its lowest living branch took off as the new upward trunk.

When you reach the loop portion of the trail, go left. Shortly before the trail cuts through the stand of rhododendrons, there is a very large, old beech on the left. To the right, there was also a large, old-growth white oak that has since died. A number of the old white oak in this stand have smooth patch disease—a condition in which portions of their outer bark are consumed by a fungus, leaving a so-called patch of smoother consistency. The fungus only consumes dead bark and doesn't harm the tree at all; it is quite common on older white oak.

▲ Two beech trees that grew close together and grafted to each at their bases. The elbow on the left shows where the lowest branch of the left tree took over as the upward-growing trunk when the original trunk was bent.

After you pass through the rhododendrons, the forest composition changes to mostly beech with some scattered white oaks. There are no red maples, red oaks, or black gums. This portion of the forest is also not as old as the previous section. Whoever planted the rhododendron also managed this part of the woodland to create a parklike beech stand. Because the trail appears to be an old carriage road, I'm guessing this part of the forest was managed for esthetics. The beech here are stunning, with their flawless, smooth bark. I am so used to seeing beech damaged by beech bark scale disease, encountering trees

▲ Smooth patch disease on the lower trunk bark of this white oak only consumes dead bark, so is not harming the tree.

like this is quite moving. Beech is our only tree to retain a smooth, esthetically gorgeous, light gray bark, and it is strikingly different from all our other trees. The beauty it added to our New England woodlands has been all but lost with this disease. Happily, that is not the case here in the Oakland Forest.

Since the bark of a beech tree doesn't develop the typical texture of other trees, it is not possible to estimate the age of a beech

Disease-free beech trees on the left and right showcase their elegant, classic, smooth gray bark. ▸

by simple observation. I was once in Pisgah State Park in New Hampshire and came to a beech that had fallen across the trail. It was a little more than a foot in diameter and someone had cut and removed a section of the trunk blocking the trail. I started counting the annual growth rings on a section of the trunk and was shocked to find that the tree was 180 years old. If someone had asked me how old I thought a beech of that size was, I would have guessed 60 years. Since beech is our most shade-tolerant hardwood, it can grow in deep shade slowly, and do fine. Beech trees can reach 350 years of age in New England.

After traversing this managed section of forest, you will cross back through the rhododendron to the intact old-growth stand. On the left will be a large red oak. Farther down the trail will be more old beech and white oaks. I was in this section of forest in November, and in the distance I saw an understory of trees retaining red leaves. I was baffled by what species it was, not having seen anything like it in a New England forest. Eventually the trail came closer and I saw that the trees were Japanese maple—a non-native species that are becoming invasive in this forest. I hope the Aquidneck Land Trust works to remove the maples, because this old-growth stand is so unique to New England that it should be kept in a natural state.

▲ This healthy, large beech is likely quite old.

▲ An old white oak stands to the right of an old beech.

▲ A trail cuts through the belt of rhododendrons, leading from one portion of the forest to the other.

▴ The red maple here is almost completely covered in poison ivy vines.

◂ The red leaves of non-native Japanese maple fill the understory of old-growth trees.

Soon you will return to the junction with the trail that will take you back to the meadow. Just before this junction, there is a red maple on the left whose trunk is covered in poison ivy vines. The vines reminded me of strangler fig trees I have seen in the tropical forest of the Amazon. These figs grow over a host tree, in time completely covering the host with its own growth and killing it. The trunks of these figs have a hollow core, where the host tree used to be. Here at Oakland Forest, the poison ivy won't kill the maple. As a climbing vine, it usually is well behaved, staying on the trunk and not growing into a tree's canopy. This makes sense, because if its host tree lives longer, the poison ivy will live longer and reproduce more. With the exception of grape vines that can kill their host tree, all our other native vines have evolved to stay on their host tree's trunk.

TILLINGHAST POND

Evidence of farming; trees shaped by extreme wind

DIFFICULTY
Moderate

LOCATION ▸ West Greenwich, Rhode Island
FEATURES FOCUS ▸ Grafting, pillows and cradles, stone walls and early agriculture, tipped trees, white pine weevil

LENGTH
2.5 miles

The Tillinghast Pond Management Area is a large holding—over 2000 acres—of The Nature Conservancy and serves as the largest block of protected land in Rhode Island. This exploration takes place on the Flintlock Loop Trail, which has generally good footing and some gain in elevation.

From the trailhead parking lot on Plain Road, head into the woods along the south side of Tillinghast Pond. You will start in a stand of weevil-hit white pines that grew after a logging of white pine around 1960. Scattered through the forest, the old stumps of the logged pines are still visible. The trail will soon come to a stone wall. If you look at the ground on the side of the stone wall facing Plain Road, you may see a plow trough running alongside the wall, where the ground is lower. This is the result of many years of annual crop field plowing. So, we can surmise that the section of forest with the weevil-hit pines was originally a crop field. It most likely transitioned into a hayfield in the mid-1800s, when rail started bringing grain from western New York and the Ohio Valley into New England. The site was abandoned in the late 1800s and then logged for white pine around 1960.

After crossing the wall, you will enter a white pine–red oak woodland that has subtle pillows and cradles, indicating this was once a pasture. You will intersect with the Flintlock Loop Trail, blazed in yellow. Turn right onto it. In this section of the forest, there will be patches of ground carpeted with tree clubmoss. Clubmosses dominated the canopies of the world's first forests, over 300 million years ago, reaching heights of 120 feet. The subcanopies of those forests were composed of tree ferns and horsetails reaching heights of about 80 feet. In those ancient forests,

A stone wall with a plow trough running next to it on the side with the blazed tree. ▸

insects also got large—dragonflies had wingspans close to 5 feet and stocky salamander-like amphibians grew to over 400 pounds. Whenever a taxonomic group comes to dominate world ecosystems, they grow to all sizes to occupy open niches.

However, when global environmental change happens quickly, the large species often go extinct. This is because large species take longer to reach sexual maturity, so they reproduce slower and can't adapt as fast. They also require more resources that become very limited in changing environments. Small species that reproduce quickly and need far fewer resources often make it through, though. The event that removed the large clubmosses, ferns, horsetails, insects, and amphibians was the Permian-Triassic Extinction that happened 252 million years ago. That event extinguished over 90 percent of marine species and about 70 percent of terrestrial species, making it the most dramatic extinction event for which we have evidence. It is not exactly clear what brought on this extinction event, but there is evidence of three separate developments that either singly or in combination may have been responsible. These include evidence of big meteor strikes and volcanic eruptions that would have thrown a lot of dust into the atmosphere, blocking solar gain and causing a large die-off of plant life. There is also evidence of oceanic microorganisms

▲ Tree clubmoss covers the forest floor.

▲ The Ellis family cemetery, near their 19th-century homestead.

releasing large amounts of methane that could have induced dramatic global warming.

The trail will become entrenched, indicating it is an old road that has eroded over the years. It will pass through a large rock wall and enter a forest with old pitch pines and an understory of dense black huckleberry. In this forest, you will also see many dead and downed oaks, killed by repeated gypsy moth outbreaks back in the 1980s. The downed oaks tipped over, popping out of the ground after their roots became just nubs. You will then come to another stone fence on the left and then the Ellis family cemetery on the right. This graveyard was active from the early to mid-1800s. After the cemetery, enter an area recently abandoned, around 2006. This was discerned by counting the limb whorls (branch layers) of the young white pines.

This site also has a lot of invasive species, including autumn olive, multiflora rose, and Eurasian bittersweet. The trail eventually leads to a dammed pond, a mill site—below the dam on the eastern side of the stream—and the Ellis homestead. Just before crossing the stream, the Flintlock Loop Trail, on which you will continue, turns to the left.

The forest on the right side of the trail has a weevil-hit white pine with many low branches, indicating that it grew by itself in the open. Soon after, the Flintlock Loop Trail will join with the Wickaboxet Loop Trail. You will go straight at this junction to stay on the Flintlock Loop Trail. It will cross two stone walls; after the

▲ An open-grown white pine with many large, low limbs. This tree grew unhindered in an open area.

second, look to the left for a swerving white pine. This pine was tipped by winds from the east in the early 1980s, by either a hurricane or a nor'easter. We can date this event via the limb near the base of the tree that grew up to be its second trunk after the tree was tipped. It had 35 to 40 limb whorls (layers).

Soon the Flintlock Loop Trail will turn to the left to depart from the Wickaboxet Loop Trail. This section of the forest has some pitch pine and a lot of pine seedlings in the understory, most likely from turkeys scratching the ground while feeding and creating exposed soil for the pine seeds to successfully establish. Cross another large stone wall and you'll enter a young forest of white pine, red oak, and some black gum, as well as highbush blueberry and black huckleberry in the understory. This site also has a lot of standing dead oak and pine. Normally I would think this section of forest had experienced a wildfire that killed a number of the trees and allowed the blueberry and hackberry to increase their density. The problem with that scenario is that none of the oak trees stump sprouted, which they would have done after their trunks were heat killed. The only other possibility is that this forest was repeatedly defoliated by gypsy moth caterpillars. Their densities were high enough that they also went after white pines, which they will do when they have eaten all the leaves of hardwood trees. By counting the limb whorls on the young white pines that came in after the event, it looks like the gypsy moth outbreak likely occurred around 2005.

As you pass through this forest, you will climb a bit and come to a junction with a small loop trail. If you go left, you will pass a number of large glacial boulders. When you come to the next junction, head left to continue on the Flintlock Loop Trail and enter another section of forest dramatically impacted by gypsy moths. On some of the boulders next to the trail, you can find nice colonies of lichens—including one called common toadskin lichen because of the bumpy nature of its grayish surface. If it's a dry day and you have some water you can spare, pour a little on the toadskin lichen and watch it change color right before your eyes.

Some sections of this oak forest have been almost completely killed by the gypsy moth and will be converted to pine forest. Soon the trail will descend

▲ Tipped by winds out of the east in the early 1980s, this white pine's lowest branch became a second trunk, growing straight up.

▲ Common toadskin lichen covers this boulder.

a bit to an older forest with a closed crown. You will then come to the junction with Tillinghast Pond Loop Trail; go left to stay on the Flintlock Loop Trail that runs with Tillinghast Pond Loop Trail for a while. Keep an eye out for rocks piled on boulders. This indicates you are entering a former crop field that was to the upslope of the

▴ Young pines grow under a canopy that has many dead oaks and pines, likely from gypsy moth defoliations.

trail. Downslope there are too many surficial rocks, meaning that the area was never a crop field. However, when the trail enters this lower area that was not a crop field, scattered in it are more rock piles. Like the stone piles that I mentioned in the chapter on Elders Grove in Massachusetts, I can't explain the presence of these piles here.

Moving through this site, you will come to a large glacial boulder that has a fine covering of moss, lichens, and even a little rock polypody fern. You might be tempted to climb this boulder, but that would negatively impact this beautiful outcrop community—it simply can't tolerate being stepped on.

After this boulder, a side trail to Phebe's Grove heads off to the right, but you will continue straight. The area will be free of all rocks,

‹ Stones piled on boulders like this usually suggest the area was cleared for a crop field, but uncleared stones nearby imply otherwise. The pile remains a mystery.

‹ A large glacial boulder with a beautiful outcrop community composed of moss, lichen, and a bit of rock polypody fern.

▲ An unusual formation: this white oak had two trunks that grafted together. The section of one of the trunks below the graft is now gone.

smooth and even, indicating a former crop field or hayfield, where plowing removed its pillows and cradles. Keep an eye to the right for a white oak that had two trunks. The trunks grew into each other and grafted together. Then something killed a section of one of the trunks below the graft—possibly it was cut away. Now the tree has a single trunk with a short section of the other trunk growing downward from it. This is a rather unusual growth form for a tree. After this tree, you will cross a stone wall with lots of small rocks, indicating that the flat ground you just passed through was once a crop field.

Soon you will come to the end of the Flintlock Loop Trail and will turn right to head back to the trailhead. About 40 feet before this trail ends, look for a live, root-grafted white pine stump in the middle of the trail. The tree was cut because it was in the way, but root grafts to neighboring pines have kept the stump alive, based on the callus that has started to grow over it.

BARKHAMSTED
+

CATHEDRAL PINES   HENRY BUCK ROAD

(8)

+
CORNWALL

+
TORRINGTON   HARTFORD

(91)

EAST WALLINGFORD +

TYLER MILL MEMORIAL

(8)

+
NEW HAVEN

CONNECTICUT

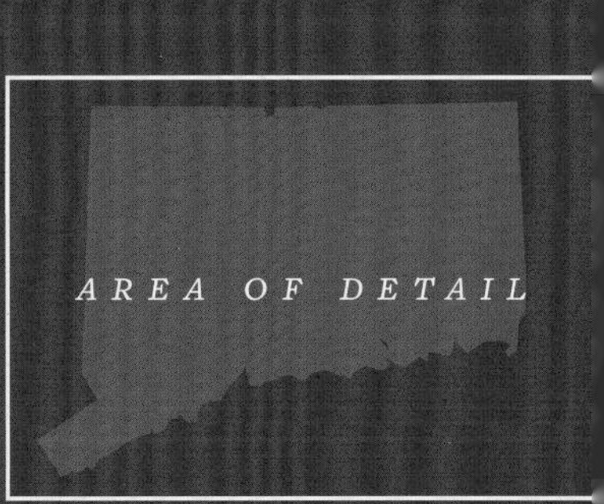

91

AREA OF DETAIL

TYLER MILL PRESERVE

Storm-impacted forest; a scenic
traprock ridge trail

DIFFICULTY
Difficult

LENGTH
2 miles

LOCATION ▸ East Wallingford, Connecticut
FEATURES FOCUS ▸ Basal fire scars, grafting, pillows and cradles, stone walls and early agriculture, tipped trees

This loop trail has a number of climbs and irregular footing on portions of the traprock ridge it traverses. For those not comfortable with exposed heights, the traprock ridge portion of this loop may be challenging.

Tyler Mill Preserve is probably best known as a mecca for regional mountain bikers. However, its traprock ridge and adjacent forests are ecologically very interesting. The preserve was closed for a time after portions of it were heavily impacted by a severe storm that hit in May 2018. Evidence of this storm can be seen throughout the hike, particularly on the southern portion of the ridge that took the brunt of it.

Traprock is a type of igneous rock, fine grained and dark. The traprock ridges here are composed of basalt and were formed in a rift valley 200 million years ago. As the valley was stretched, faults formed, molten magma flowed into them, then cooled to form basalt intrusions. As erosion removed the sandstone in which the intrusions occurred, erosion-resistant traprock ridges were left rising steeply from the surrounding landscape. The one in the Tyler Mill Preserve is small compared to others. It rises 100 feet or so from the surrounding terrain, and the knife-edged portions of its ridgeline drop steeply on both sides.

This exploration starts on Lilac Trail, which begins in a moderately sloping hayfield. After about 100 meters, the trail crosses a stone wall composed of small rocks and enters an oak woodland. The ground in this forest is smooth and even, and there are extracted, fist-sized rocks in the adjacent stone wall, indicating that this was at one time a crop field. Additional support for this theory is the close proximity of the forest/field to the traprock ridge, because basalt weathers into fine, nutrient-enriched soil. A short way into this woodland, the trail crosses a red oak dropped by the 2018 storm. About 40 feet above the ground, this oak forked. When it was blown over, the base of the fork hit directly on the trunk of another oak; the force of its fall split the toppled oak right down the middle of its trunk all the way to its root system. If this oak is allowed to remain in place, the evidence of its demise should still be visible a good 60 years from now.

When you come to the junction with the Orange Trail, go left. The trail will switchback as it climbs up the northern end of the traprock ridge. The forest changes from oak to one composed of pignut hickory, hemlock, and eastern red cedar. Eastern red cedars are a common component on Connecticut's traprock ridges. If not overtopped by other trees, they can grow quite old—up to 300 years of age.

▲ When it was blown over in 2018, this red oak hit another tree and split completely in half.

Soon the ridge becomes an edge—only a bit more than 10 feet wide on the top. Farther on, that width will diminish to 4 feet, with both sides dropping steeply to the forest below.

Keep an eye on the left side of the trail for a hemlock that was tipped over by weight and most likely cleared from the trail. Today it is a bent stump about 4 feet in length, still alive because it is root grafted to the hemlock growing next to it. Based on the amount of callus wood growing over the wound, this hemlock was bent sometime around 1980. The hemlocks on this ridge are pretty beat up because of exposure to storms, and are older than their size suggests.

▲ The ridgetop becomes quite narrow, falling dramatically on both sides.

Soon the trail will start to descend into a small col (valley) on the ridgeline. As it does, you can see a sugar maple on the right, tipped over by winds coming from the east, most likely from a tropical storm or hurricane that impacted this site around 1990. The maple's lowest limb took over as the new trunk, and the original downed trunk died and decayed away. It is possible that the bent hemlock and downed sugar maple are the result of the same storm, possibly Hurricane Gloria in 1985. If not, it means that two storms with strong winds from the east occurred in this part of the state in the late 1900s.

▲ A hemlock bent over by weight around 1980; it is still alive thanks to a root graft to a neighboring hemlock.

At the bottom of the col, you will come to the junction with the Red Trail. Take a left to stay on the Orange Trail. It will rise on switchbacks to the next portion of the ridge. There are a number of dead hemlock trees in this part of the forest, most likely killed by the hemlock wooly adelgid—an exotic, sap-sucking insect from Asia. This species was first seen in Connecticut in 1985. It is believed

▲ This sugar maple was blown over by strong winds from the east, then the lowest limb took over as the trunk and grew upward.

that it was carried from Long Island into the state by the winds of Hurricane Gloria. What is encouraging about this population of hemlocks at Tyler Mill is that many of the trees are alive, and show no presence of the white, wooly insects on the trees' fine twigs. This means that either some of the hemlocks have resistance to the adelgid or that the dead hemlocks were killed by something else. My guess is the former, because the adelgid is quite prevalent around this part of Connecticut, and can disperse quickly. As you begin to crest the ridge, you may see that moss becomes prominent on both sides of the trail.

Along the top of this portion of the ridge you will come to a stunted dead hemlock on the right that had large, low limbs growing near the ground. This tree grew in the open all by itself for many

▲ Moss becomes prevalent along the trail as it crests the ridge after the first col.

years and took on an unusual growth form for a hemlock. Just after this hemlock, as the trail begins to descend, look downslope on the left to see a number of trees with uphill basal scars created by a fire that burned up this eastern facing slope.

After the fire-scarred trees, the trail makes a steep descent into the second col on the ridgeline, and then a steep ascent to the next crest of the ridge. As the trail levels out, there is a 6-inch-diameter black birch on the left with a hole in the base of its trunk. Based on its bark, this tree is in the range of 150 to 200 years of age—an indication of the tough growing conditions on this dry ridgetop. Farther down the trail, you will come to an old chestnut oak that has a lightning scar spiraling to the right up its trunk. After this oak, you will enter a portion of the preserve that was heavily impacted by the 2018 storm.

Although tornados were a part of the storm system that impacted this part of Connecticut in May 2018, it looks to me like this section of the Tyler Mill Preserve was hit by a microburst. All the

▴ Uphill basal fire scars appear on trees to the left of the trail.

▴ An old lightning scar spirals up a chestnut oak.

trees fell in the same direction from winds coming out of the west. Even if it wasn't a tornado, it was still a devastating storm on this section of the ridge, with downed trees and tip-ups (uprooted tree bases and root masses) everywhere. Luckily, the hike doesn't end with this as the last thing you see. Descending from the ridge, you will enter an intact forest with old chestnut oaks.

Heading toward the road, you will come to a junction with the Red Trail. Take a right onto this trail, and cross a stone wall that also has posts strung with barbed wire. The wire means that a pasture used to be on at least one side of this wall. The ground on the far side of the wall has pillows and cradles, a number of old oak stumps, and coppiced chestnut oaks. Some of these coppiced chestnut oaks are quite large and old. Farther down the trail, on the right side, is a chestnut oak with four trunks. Each of those trunks is almost 2 feet in diameter, suggesting that this tree was cut during the second half of the 1800s. The original trunk would have also been close to 2 feet in diameter, indicating its acorn germinated in the late 1700s. The old oak suggests that its side of the fence has always been forested, so the pasture was likely on the side of the fence toward the road.

The trail then runs between the base of the traprock ridge to its right and a red maple swamp to its left. At the base of the ridge, you will find talus slopes lying below cliffs that rise to the ridgetop. The forest close to the swamp has a lot of hemlock and yellow birch, indicating a cool, moist microenvironment adjacent to the swamp.

Eventually you will come adjacent to the first col on the ridgeline. A spur of Red Trail goes up to connect with the Orange Trail there. At this juncture, go left. In time, the forest will change from hemlocks to oaks and hickories. When you come to the intersection with the Yellow Trail, go right and onto it. This will take you to the junction with the Orange Trail, onto which you will turn right again. Switchback up and over a hill to at last come back to the Lilac Trail. Turn left onto the Lilac Trail, and head back down to the parking area.

▲ A section of the ridge devastated by the 2018 storm.

▲ A large coppiced chestnut oak with four trunks was probably cut in the second half of the 1800s. It first sprouted in the late 1700s.

HENRY BUCK TRAIL

Old-growth hardwoods, including a 6-foot-diameter white ash

DIFFICULTY	Difficult

LOCATION ▸ Barkhamsted, Connecticut
FEATURES FOCUS ▸ Old growth, pillows and cradles, stone walls and early agriculture

LENGTH	2 miles

Sections of steep uphill climbing, some irregular footing, and the length of this round-trip hike make it best undertaken by those prepared for such terrain and conditions. That said, the Henry Buck Trail in the American Legion State Forest is, in my experience, the best-developed nutrient-enriched, old-growth, hardwood forest in the state of Connecticut. The bulk of the old growth is uphill from the trail on an east-facing talus slope, similar to the Todd-Clark woodland in the Mohawk Trail State Forest of Massachusetts. However, sections of this trail run alongside and then into the old-growth stand.

Start on the southern end of this loop trail, near an old bridge abutment on the Farmington River. The trail is named for Henry Buck, who oversaw the trail's construction by the Civilian Conservation Corps (CCC) in the 1930s.

The trail starts to climb toward the talus slope in a mixed hardwood forest. You will soon start to see big trees, including a large, 4-foot-diameter red oak to the right of the trail. Although large, the oak is not old, because its bark is quite smooth and has been stretched by the tree's fast-growing girth. I am guessing this tree is probably less than 100 years of age—a testament to the favorable growing conditions of this site. Continuing up the trail, you will come to boulders carpeted in moss and rock polypody (a type of fern that grows on rocks). The bedrock on this site is calcium enriched and has given rise to productive forest soils.

▲ A fast-growing, 4-foot-diameter red oak. The smoothness of the bark indicates it has been stretched by accelerated growth.

▲ Moss-covered boulders here support rock polypody fern.

At the crest of the first climb there is another large red oak on the left and upslope to the right is the start of the old-growth trees, including beech, sugar maple, and some large white ash. The trail then levels out and enters a younger hardwood forest of bitternut hickory and basswood—two calcium-loving trees that attest to the site's rich soils. A look at the ground will show it is smooth, with no surficial rocks. This indicates is was a former hayfield or crop field, where plowing removed its pillows and cradles.

Here, the trail runs right along the lower edge of the talus slope, with large boulders to its right and no boulders to its left. On the right, you will come to the largest tree along the trail—a huge, 6-foot-diameter white ash. This is without a doubt the largest forest-grown white ash I have ever seen. Uphill, the old growth is well established, with lots of sugar maple, beech, and bitternut hickory. The bark of bitternut hickory looks like that of white ash, except it is much smoother. It has the same cantaloupe rind pattern, but bitternut hickory's bark fissures are much shallower. In the understory of the old growth is a lot of mountain maple—a small tree that thrives on talus slopes.

Eventually the trail passes through a downed hemlock and enters an area with numerous hemlocks deformed by porcupine browsing. Many of these trees have forked trunks with large, low limbs. Some are missing tops. This is a perfect spot for porcupines, with boulder caves in the talus for den sites and the mammal's favorite browse species—hemlock—nearby. After the smaller, deformed trees, the trail will pass between two much older hemlocks that are at least 200 years of age. Then the trail enters the boulders of the talus slope.

As you climb up the talus field, the hemlocks are left behind and replaced by old-growth hardwoods due to the enrichment coming from the boulders. At first the trail is a rock stairway that gives way to very irregular footing on the boulders. For anyone without excellent balance this would be the time to turn back; it would be easy to take a fall here. Continuing up, you will find some old-growth white ash to the right and another section of deformed hemlocks.

As the trail nears the ridgetop, the slope begins to be exposed to western winds and the old growth disappears due to lack of wind protection. At this point the trail starts to switchback up the slope and encounters more deformed hemlocks. You will then hit another section of rock stairs followed by more switchbacks until you come to a ledge outcropping where the trail

▲ Old-growth sugar maples populate the talus slope above the trail.

▲ My wife stands next to a 6-foot-diameter white ash: the largest I have ever seen.

turns left and enters the much-younger forest on the ridgetop. At this point I turned around to head back down. However, the trail crosses the ridge and heads back down to the road about a quarter mile north of where you started. If you decide to continue on, you will do some scrambling along the cliff face that lies above the talus slope.

▲ Hardwood old growth in the talus slope.

▲ Hemlocks like this one are deformed in this area because of frequent porcupine browsing.

▲ Rock stairs climb through the talus.

▲ Two old white ash trees in the talus slope.

CATHEDRAL PINES PRESERVE

Once 40 acres of old-growth white pine; still awe inspiring today

DIFFICULTY
Moderate

LOCATION ▸ Cornwall, Connecticut
FEATURES FOCUS ▸ Old growth, pillows and cradles, stone walls and early agriculture

LENGTH
1 mile

This is a round-trip hike with two hill climbs and generally good footing. Parking at the trailhead is quite limited.

The Cathedral Pines was an old-growth stand of white pine that covered about 40 acres. It was devastated by a blowdown in 1989. That line of thunderstorms generated tornados; however, because all the downed pines at this site lie in the same direction, it makes me think that this blowdown may have been from a microburst and not a tornado. There is still a small pocket of old-growth pine and hemlock as well as some other interesting features here, all of which make this a worthwhile hike.

The land parcel was bought in 1883 by the Calhoun family. They did so to protect the pines—which at that time were already over a century old. In doing so, the family distinguished themselves as very early preservationists. In 1967, the Calhouns donated the parcel to The Nature Conservancy. Following the blowdown, rather than salvaging the valuable timber, the conservancy chose to leave it as a site for studying forest dynamics and ecological succession.

You will be taking the blue-blazed Mohawk Trail into the site. Right at the start, look for many large, downed white pines, all lying in the same direction and dropped by winds from the west. These trees have shed their bark and their trunks are coated in moss. In time, small-seeded black birch and hemlock will germinate in this moss and the pines will become nurse logs. In 2200, a person who

▲ Large, downed white pines all lie in the same direction, toppled by a 1989 blowdown.

▲ This small stand of old-growth white pine survived the 1989 storm.

knows how to interpret blowdowns will be able to walk into this site and surmise that a historic thunderstorm blew down many very large white pines. How will they be able to do this, if by that time all these downed pines will have completely decayed away? They will know it was a thunderstorm by the strength of the winds that came out of the west, based on the orientation of the pillows and cradles. By the size of the pillows and cradles, they will be able to tell the trees were very big. The rows of stilted-root black birch and hemlock trees will reveal that these trees grew on nurse logs—and the only tree species in Connecticut that makes good nurse logs is white pine.

The trail then switchbacks up a slope and enters a small stand of old-growth white pines that survived the storm. Downslope from the trail, look for a pine snag whose trunk snapped off during the storm but didn't uproot. A little farther on, upslope from the trail, is an old-growth hemlock with chartreuse-green lichen on its bark—a type of lichen that I haven't seen grow on bark until the tree is more than 275 years of age. The trail then turns left and continues to climb. The forest on this hill was surprisingly spared by the storm.

Approaching the top of the hill, look to the left for a white pine snag—standing next to an old pine—that has advanced decay at the base of its trunk. This is called a rot collar and it develops on standing dead trees. Eventually the decay will get so extensive that the snag will snap off at that point and fall to the ground. Most standing

▴ This white pine trunk snapped but didn't uproot when hit by the storm's winds.

▴ Rot collars form at the base of standing dead trees, such as this white pine.

▴ A black birch grows on the tip-up of a downed tree.

▴ A large pillow and cradle in the making.

dead trees fall in this fashion. The exception is oak, whose roots decay before a rot collar can form. Once their roots are gone, oaks simply pop out of the ground. Farther on you will see evidence of a deadfall hemlock that snapped off at its rot collar. For decay to develop, moisture is needed. The rotting roots of a dead tree wick water up to the base of its trunk, allowing for faster decay and the development of rot collars. Hikers should know that it may be unsafe to be in the woods on very windy days; the same is true for heavy rain events. Most snags absorb water and when the weight increases enough, the tree can snap off without warning.

▲ A barway between a pasture and crop field allows access.

▲ This deadfall hemlock broke off at its rot collar.

▲ Rock walls for pastures are composed mostly of big rocks, because the land wasn't plowed for crops, only cleared of the largest obstructions.

▲ A small stone pile on the right side of the barway. Small and large rocks were removed from crop fields to prepare them for cultivation.

The ground on this hill is even, so we can assume it was once plowed for crops or hay, which removed the pillows and cradles it would otherwise have. There are pines close to 200 years of age on this hill, indicating this part of the parcel was abandoned in the early 1800s.

Crest the hill and you will descend into a ravine. Beginning your ascent out of the ravine, you will reenter the blowdown. The climb up is steep but short. As you come out of the ravine, look to your right for a black birch growing from the tip-up (base and root mass) of a downed tree. Farther on, you will come to a large pillow and cradle being created on the right. The trail will start to level out, then make a turn to the right. After this turn, look for a hemlock on the right that snapped off from its rot collar in 2019.

Past the deadfall hemlock, you will enter a former pasture with large rock walls and uneven ground. The trail then passes through a barway in one of the pasture walls and enters a former crop field. This can be discerned by the smooth, even ground on the far side of the wall and the small stone pile on the right side of the barway. Here you will leave the Cathedral Pines Preserve. Time to turn around and head back to the trailhead.

LIST OF SPECIES

Trees

Speckled alder + *Alnus incana*

Apple + *Malus domestica*

American mountain ash + *Sorbus americana*

Black ash + *Fraxinus nigra*

Green ash + *Fraxinus pennsylvanica*

White ash + *Fraxinus americana*

Bigtooth aspen + *Populus grandidentata*

Quaking aspen + *Populus tremuloides*

Basswood + *Tilia americana*

American beech + *Fagus grandifolia*

Black birch + *Betula lenta*

Gray birch + *Betula populifolia*

Paper birch + *Betula papyrifera*

Yellow birch + *Betula alleghaniensis*

Eastern red cedar + *Juniperus virginiana*

Northern white cedar + *Thuja occidentalis*

Black cherry + *Prunus serotina*

American chestnut + *Castanea dentata*

Eastern cottonwood + *Populus deltoides*

Box elder + *Acer negundo*

American elm + *Ulmus americana*

Balsam fir + *Abies balsamea*

Douglas fir + *Pseudotsuga menziesii*

Hackberry + *Celtis occidentalis*

Eastern hemlock + *Tsuga canadensis*

Bitternut hickory + *Carya cordiformis*

Pignut hickory + *Carya glabra*

Shagbark hickory + *Carya ovata*

Hop hornbeam + *Ostrya virginiana*

Larch + *Larix laricina*

Black locust + *Robinia pseudoacacia*

Japanese maple + *Acer palmatum*

Mountain maple + *Acer spicatum*

Red maple + *Acer rubrum*

Silver maple + *Acer saccharinum*

Striped maple + *Acer pensylvanicum*

Sugar maple + *Acer saccharum*

Musclewood + *Carpinus caroliniana*

Bear oak + *Quercus ilicifolia*

Black oak + *Quercus velutina*

Bur oak + *Quercus macrocarpa*

Chestnut oak + *Quercus prinus*

Red oak + *Quercus rubra*

Swamp white oak + *Quercus bicolor*

White oak + *Quercus alba*

Jack pine + *Pinus banksiana*

Pitch pine + *Pinus rigida*

Red pine + *Pinus resinosa*

White pine + *Pinus strobus*

Coast redwood + *Sequoia sempervirens*

Sassafras + *Sassafras albidum*

Black spruce + *Picea mariana*

Red spruce + *Picea rubens*

American sycamore + *Plantanus occidentalis*

Tulip tree + *Liriodendron tulipifera*

Shrubs and Vines

Trailing arbutus + *Epigaea repens*

Alpina azalea + *Kalmia procumbens*

Northern bayberry + *Myrica pensylvanica*

Bearberry + *Arctostaphylos uva-ursi*

Bog bilberry + *Vaccinium uliginosum*

Eurasian bittersweet + *Celastrus scandens*

Highbush blueberry + *Vaccinium corymbosum*

Lowbush blueberry + *Vaccinium angustifolium*

Checkerberry + *Gaultheria procumbens*

Mountain cranberry + *Vaccinium vitis-idaea*

Small cranberry + *Vaccinium oxycoccos*

Black crowberry + *Empetrum nigrum*

Broom crowberry + *Corema conradii*

Diapensia + *Diapensia lapponica*

Sweet fern + *Comptonia peregrina*

Mountain heather + *Phyllodoce caerulea*

Sand heather + *Hudsonia tomentosa*

Hobblebush + *Viburnum lantanoides*

Winterberry holly + *Ilex verticillata*

Black huckleberry + *Gaylussacia baccata*

Wild grape + *Vitis* species

Greenbriar + *Smilax rotundifolia*

Inkberry + *Ilex glabra*

Poison ivy + *Toxicodendron radicans*

Labrador tea + *Rhododendron groenlandicum*

Bog laurel + *Kalmia polifolia*

Mountain laurel + *Kalmia latifolia*

Sheep laurel + *Kalmia angustifolia*

Leatherleaf + *Chamaedaphne calyculata*

Autumn olive + *Elaeagnus umbellata*

Great rhododendron + *Rhododendron maximum*

Rhodora + *Rhododendron canadense*

Multiflora rose + *Rosa multiflora*

Lapland rosebay + *Rhododendron lapponicum*

Bog rosemary + *Andromeda polifolia*

Spotted wintergreen + *Chimaphila maculata*

Herbaceous Plants

Mountain avens + *Geum peckii*

Baneberry + *Actaea* species

Alpine bluet + *Houstonia caerulea*

Skunk cabbage + *Symplocarpus foetidus*

Tree clubmoss + *Dendrolycopodium dendroideum*

Blue cohosh + *Caulophyllum thalictroides*

Red columbine + *Aquilegia canadensis*

Cotton grass + *Eriophorum* species

Dutchman's breeches + *Dicentra cucullaria*

American dunegrass + *Leymus mollis*

Cinnamon fern + *Osmundastrum cinnamomeum*

Maidenhair fern + *Adiantum pedatum*

Maidenhair spleenwort + *Asplenium trichomanes*

Rock polypody fern + *Polypodium virginianum*

Royal fern + *Osmunda regalis*

Walking fern + *Asplenium rhizophyllum*

Grass pink + *Calopogon tuberosus*

Wild ginger + *Asarum canadense*

False hellebore + *Veratrum viride*

Round-lobed hepatica + *Hepatica americana*

Herb Robert + *Geranium robertianum*

Wild leek + *Allium tricoccum*

Calla lily + *Zantedeschia aethiopica*

Trout lily + *Erythronium americanum*

Indian pipe + *Monotropa uniflora*

Pitcher plant + *Sarracenia purpurea*

Downy rattlesnake plantain + *Goodyera pubescens*

Bigelow's sedge + *Carex bigelowii*

Plantain-leaved sedge + *Carex plantaginea*

Pennsylvania sedge + *Carex pensylvanica*

Spring beauty + *Claytonia virginica*

Squirrel corn + *Dicentra canadensis*

Round-leaved sundew + *Drosera rotundifolia*

Red trillium + *Trillium erectum*

Roundleaf yellow violet + *Viola rotundifolia*

Lichens and Moss

Alpine reindeer lichen + *Cladonia stellaris*

Cinder lichen + *Aspicilia cinerea*

Common reindeer lichen + *Cladonia rangiferina*

Common toadskin lichen + *Lasallia papulosa*

Green reindeer lichen + *Cladonia mitis*

Maritime sunburst lichen + *Xanthoria parietina*

Target lichen + *Arctoparmelia centrifuga*

Usnea + *Usnea* species

Haircap moss + *Polytrichum commune*

Sphagnum + *Sphagnum* species

Mammals

Beaver + *Castor canadensis*

Gray squirrel + *Sciurus carolinensis*

Porcupine + *Erethizon dorsatum*

Birds

Ruby-throated hummingbird + *Archilochus colubris*

Yellow-bellied sapsucker + *Sphyrapicus varius*

Tree swallow + *Tachycineta bicolor*

Turkey + *Meleagris gallopavo*

Pileated woodpecker + *Dryocopus pileatus*

Insects

Hemlock woolly adelgid + *Adelges tsugae*

Carpenter ants + *Camponotus* species

Allegheny mound ants + *Formica exsectoides*

Pleasing fungus beetle + *Megalodacne* species

Beech scale + *Cryptococcus fagisuga*

Acorn weevil + *Curculio glandium*

White pine weevil + *Pissodes strobi*

Fungi

Chestnut blight + *Cryphonectria parasitica*

Earthstar + *Scleroderma* species

Hemlock shelf fungus + *Ganoderma tsugae*

Neonectria + *Neonectria* species

Smooth patch disease + *Aleurodiscus oakesii*

ACKNOWLEDGMENTS

I first need to thank Stacee Lawrence for reaching out to me to see if I would be interested in writing a book on the natural history of New England for Timber Press. Another person at Timber that I need to thank is Julie Talbot for doing such a great job as the editor of my manuscript. Thanks also to the many people who suggested sites that I should consider. In Vermont, Matt Kolan mentioned Kingsland Bay State Park. In Massachusetts, both Ray Asselin and Bob Leverett suggested the sites in the western part of the state covered in this book. Clair Cain, Eric Hammerling, and Peter Rzasa mentioned sites in Connecticut. Kyle Turoczi—a former teaching assistant of mine at Antioch—drew my attention to the Henry Buck Trail and the Tyler Mill Preserve—two sites I was not familiar with that were both important additions. In Rhode Island, both Fern Graves and Mark Temblay suggested the Tillinghast Pond Management Area. Finally, my deepest gratitude to my wife Marcia, who traveled with me across New England to explore these wonderful places.

INDEX

TOM WESSELS is a terrestrial ecologist and professor emeritus at Antioch University New England where he founded the master's degree program in conservation biology. With interests in forest, desert, arctic, and alpine ecosystems, plus geomorphology, evolutionary ecology, complex systems science, and the interface of landscape and culture, Tom considers himself a generalist. He has conducted workshops on ecology and sustainability throughout the country for over three decades and is the author of numerous books on these subjects.